To two wonderful happ[illegible] people, John [illegible]ill.

Thank you for your support over the past few years.

Rachel x.

Happy Silver People

How to make life happier as you grow older

Rachel Woodward Carrick

This is a work of non-fiction based on the experiences and recollections of the author, with some minor changes which do not affect the substantial accuracy of the work. Names of some individuals have been changed. This book is not intended to be a substitute for the advice of health professionals, and the reader should seek medical guidance for health-related matters.

First edition independently published by Happy Silver People Books in the United Kingdom 2022.

A CIP catalogue record of this book is available from the British Library.

ISBN (Hardcover): 978-1-3999-3449-7
ISBN (Paperback): 979-8-8475-1046-2
Typeset by Matthew J Bird

For further information about this book, please contact the author at happysilverpeople@yahoo.com or through the Happy Silver People website.

Dedication

To lovely Laura
May you always be happy,
and one day be silver.

To Mum, James, and Rob
Now you are silver,
may you always be happy.

To Dad, Robert, and Hugh
Only one of you got to be silver,
but you all made us happy
in the time you were here.

Today is the oldest
you've ever been,
and the youngest
you'll ever be again

Eleanor Roosevelt

Contents

Foreword by Harry Redknapp

Why did I agree to do the foreword for Happy Silver People?

Well, I know Rachel has been through some tough times in her life. but she's worked hard to keep a positive mindset, and now that she's fast approaching her sixties, she's got some great ideas to share about growing older.

I remember back to when my parents were around my age. They hadn't had the benefit of being able to travel much - the furthest Mum ever travelled was from the East End of London down to Bournemouth, and the only time Dad was ever on a plane was when he flew them in the war. On a Friday night, to get a break from the big council estate we lived on, they'd head off to the caravan on the Isle of Sheppey,

How times have changed. I've had the chance to travel a lot more than they did, of course, because of football. But one of the places I'd still like to visit is Las Vegas, just for a few days to take in some of the shows. Oh, and I'd love to play a round or two of golf on the Old Course at St Andrews.

My golf and watching the horses are still things I enjoy, although I can't play tennis anymore, thanks to my knees. I think I get my love of sport from my dad. He would watch boxing, snooker, darts - any kind of game or match that was on TV. Every Saturday, he'd head off with his box of sandwiches, made by my mum, to watch Liverpool play. My mother was quite traditional and enjoyed cooking and looking after family and friends. They were very happy together.

I think it's important to be thankful for the simple, good things in life. For me, that would include walking every day and going out for dinner with Sandra. I also know just how fortunate I am to live in such lovely surroundings, near the sea and lots of green space.

I also don't have too many regrets. My greatest is that I didn't make more of my education, but the reality is that opportunities were limited. There weren't any books in the classroom, teachers would struggle and often be in tears, and kids left school without being able to read or write, although they were highly skilled at making paper aeroplanes. Instead of doing homework, we'd play football every night until it was dark, amongst the rubble on the old bomb sites.

Who inspired me in those days? The sports master at my junior school who had a passion for cricket and football. If I'd been into writing thank you letters, I would have sent one to him.

Throughout my life, I've always tried to engage with people on a personal level. Back in the day, I took time to get to know the younger players and coaches, asking them questions and giving them individual feedback. I think it's important to make the effort to stay engaged and connected with others as you grow older, to take an interest in the people and the world around you.

It's also good to be nice. I'd be happy to be remembered as someone who had time for everyone. People ask me how I put up with strangers constantly coming up to say hello and asking for photos. I like letting people feel they know me, and giving them some attention - sometimes you can make their day. My dad was the same; he'd chat to anyone.

So, while I confess to not being overjoyed at the prospect of getting too much older, I'll be bearing in mind the themes Rachel covers in this book: doing what I can to stay active, keeping my mind bright; appreciating the positives in life, and sometimes trying something new. Lebanese food, you're next on the list.

And, whatever age I reach,
I plan to be nice. Always.

Do not regret growing older.

It is a privilege denied to many.

Anon

Introduction

1. A Happy Silver Person
2. Three score years and ten

1. A Happy Silver Person

Friday 1 January 2021. We were all sailing into the uncharted waters of another new year. But more significantly for me, it was the first time I could say these momentous words,

"Next year, I will be 60."

The next stage of my life had bobbed into sight. It could be spotted through my grandpa's huge binoculars, right there on the horizon. Old age, ahoy!

Naturally, this quickly got me thinking about what was to come...

I was, of course, aware that I was moving beyond 'middle-age', and could quickly trot out a list of negatives associated with ageing. I could start with failing health, reduced finances, and an ever-expanding waistline, and then move on through fewer opportunities, loneliness, and the inexplicable attraction of yet another sunny afternoon watching repeats of Midsomer Murders in a comfy reclining chair, with my slippered feet on a matching footstool.

But surely, ageing didn't have to be all bad?

Coming towards the end of my fifties. I was not in the best shape. After some very challenging years, I found myself with no hobbies, few friends, and no idea what had happened to the 'real me'. Someone asked, "What's your favourite season?" and I found I was unable to answer.

For some time, my preferences hadn't been terribly relevant, meaning that I now had no inkling as to which time of year I liked best, how I'd like to spend my spare time, or where I wanted to go at the weekend. Plus, I felt frumpy, dumpy, and grumpy - and had eye bags to rival those of Noddy Holder. I wouldn't have minded so much if I'd had his voice to go with them.

Given where I was, in the doldrums, how was I going to navigate these important impending years? Where was the chart I needed to help me steer my way into a bold new seascape?

I quickly discovered there was no such treasure trove of information. What I found was too medical, too pastel-coloured, too depressing, or too existential for me.

I was seeking small, simple, but significant things I could do; happy-making ideas and activities which were low-cost and easily accessible. I wanted some to lead to quick wins; others to be catalysts for greater positive change in myself. I swerved to avoid overly-challenging targets with timelines, which would likely result in struggle, stress, and a sense of failure.

I would have to find the answers to these questions – and more – myself:

- What kind of older person do I want to be?
- How will I make each day fun, interesting, and engaging?
- How could I stay connected to others and the wider community?
- Which things would I like to have around me, and which could I let go?
- How do I want to be remembered?
- How can I prepare right now to make my life as happy, healthy, and easy as it can be in the future?

Nearly two years on, I'm finding that my perspective is shifting, and I can now stop striving for my idea of a perfect future that will never come. There is indeed happiness, a sense of fulfilment, even fun and excitement to be found in a new imperfect present, in between increasingly frequent hunts for my glasses and trips to the loo.

And I don't need to become a centenarian to see value in the simpler things in life, such as a smile, a starry sky, and socks that don't cut your circulation off at the calf.

Over the past eighteen months, I've been up in the crow's nest, embracing my new silver (OK, browny-greyish-white) plumage, and getting ready to hatch Happy Silver People. Passengers on the deck below include my super-special daughter, Lovely Laura, and my husband Rob, hereafter referred to as the Big Yorkshire Silverback or BYS for short (not to be confused with BTS, the Korean boyband).

The inevitable question has been asked. "Just why would anyone be interested in a book of ideas for happier ageing written by you?"

One publisher broke it to me that people only buy books like this if they're written by national treasures, or at least household names, or perhaps influencers with flocks of followers. With seventy-one YouTube subscribers which included three kind friends of my brother, I couldn't yet class myself in the category of even a ZZZ-list celebrity.

If I were suddenly transformed into a bird, I doubt it would be one that attracts attention and admiration, especially now I am enveloped in the invisibility cloak of late middle age. So, not a glamorous peacock, enchanting nightingale, or soaring condor.

I suspect I would instead be a small, silvery-brown bird. Perhaps a sparrow, alighting onto the edge of that lofty crow's nest to catch my breath.

What could anyone learn from a bird so humble, so inconspicuous, so ordinary? Well, maybe a lot!

Let me share seven sensational facts about sparrows:

- They are sociable, even gregarious, and frequently nest together in colonies
- As they've adapted to live alongside humans, they can be found just about everywhere in the world, except in deserts and forests
- They've been seen feeding on the 80th floor of the Empire State Building...
- ... and have also been spotted breeding nearly 2,000 feet underground in a Yorkshire coalmine

- Like elephants, they enjoy a good dust bath
- If they sense danger, they can swim underwater to escape
- The oldest known sparrow died aged thirteen years and four months.

It seems an everyday sparrow could show us all something about relationships, adaptability, resilience, grabbing opportunities, having fun, managing risk, and living to a ripe old age!

I aim to do the same.

This drawing was kindly given to me by Sue Trusler who discovered a passion and talent for art after retiring from a career in finance. Her first book is entitled ***Time to Start Your Art*** *and she has recently had one of her paintings electronically displayed in Times Square, New York.*

Sue fancies being a blue budgie: bright, cheerful, and chattering away. Much like Pip, her feathery friend when she was growing up.

2. Three score years and ten

"Just who are these 'Silver People' she is writing for?" you may well be wondering.

Well, although I now look the part of a Silver Person, you don't need to have silver hair - or indeed any hair - to be in this gang.

I think of Silver People as the huge tribe of us in our fifties onwards. What a fascinating and diverse group we are! Far more interesting than some of those online surveys would suggest when they ask us to declare our age:

- 20 to 29
- 30 to 39
- 40 to 49
- 50 to 59 (we know it's unlikely, but feel we have to ask)
- 60 plus (yes, we're aware this age range could span 40+ years but please appreciate our generosity in including this option at all. It's just in case one of two of you have somehow found your way to our survey; we suspect you probably meant to Google something else).

However, there is an increasing interest elsewhere in discovering more about our ever-growing group: our wants and needs; the nuances of our ambitions and passions; the myriad of opportunities that, with just a little encouragement, we might set out to explore.

Just as well, given that in the UK today there are around twenty-five million people over the age of fifty and nine million over seventy.

Many moons ago, seventy or 'threescore years and ten', would have been considered the ripest of old ages.

The Bible sets this expectation about lifespan in Psalm 90 verse 10:

- King James Bible version: The days of our years are threescore years and ten; and if by reason of strength they be fourscore years, yet is their strength labour and sorrow; for it is soon cut off, and we fly away.

- Happy Silver People translation: Many of us will live to 70. If you're a tough cookie you might live to 80, but it will be hard-going and not much fun. Don't worry, though, you won't have to struggle too long before your time comes to an end, and you fly off into the sunset.

I like those references to (old) birds flapping off into the distance and over the horizon. Much nicer than 'dropping off your perch'.

Fortunately, times have been a-changing since Moses wrote that Psalm. But while a growing group of OAPs was lucky enough to hit seventy back in the '70s, looking and behaving 'old' seemed to be part of the deal.

Formal clothes were for everyday wear, even when roasting on the beach: collars, ties, braces, and proper shoes with leather soles. Women had hats like Liquorice Allsorts, bloomers under petticoats, and handbags with clasps pursed as tight as their lips.

The oldies of my youth carried pressed handkerchiefs, mint humbugs, full-sized umbrellas, and occasionally a pipe. They suffered from lumbago and funny turns and felt things in their water.

Of my grandparents, Cyril, Beatrice, and Clifford (the proud owner of the previously mentioned massive binoculars) were born between 1890 and 1900 and, sadly, all died from ill-health in different guises in their late sixties or early seventies.

My maternal grandmother, Gwendoline (married to the owner of the colossal binoculars), was the exception. Born in 1904, she lived to one hundred and three. At the time of her birth, life expectancy in the UK had crept all the way up to fifty, but an active ninety-year-old would have been as rare as smashed avocado on sourdough toast for breakfast.

Grannie Gwen enjoying the heatwave of 1976

Nowadays the number of people who are living to one hundred (or five-score years) has reached almost half a million worldwide. There are even a few super-centenarians, who make it beyond five-score years and ten. The oldest living person, based on reliable records, was Jeanne Calment of France, who died aged 122 in 1997. At the time of writing, another long-lifer (or long-liver?) can be found in Japan, 118-year-old Kane Tanaka.

What might Grannie Gwendoline have had in her favour, which my other grandparents did not? My guess is that it was a happy blend of the following:

- No significant underlying health issues
- Being female – statistically, we live longer than men
- Not being a smoker. Ever
- Not drinking. *Almost* never. As a strict Methodist, she took a vow of temperance in her youth, although she was partial to a sneaky liqueur chocolate in her later years

- A simple diet based on wartime experience in the UK, encompassing plenty of local meat, seasonal vegetables, and homemade cakes
- Walking an awful lot – she never learned to drive
- Always being on the lookout for new adventures. She loved social events, trips, and the chance to dress up
- Lots of close contact with friends and family, especially important after being widowed in her sixties. She was always writing letters and was an active member of the church, clubs, and societies
- Feeling needed, particularly when helping out with her grandchildren and knitting copiously for others
- Her faith, which meant she didn't live in fear of the future
- Oh, and strong longevity genes too. Probably.

I've drawn on this, and my own experiences, to set out six areas of focus for this book.

And the strangest thing happened when I listed out the themes: the initial letters spell out the word SILVER. What a happy coincidence!

Stimulating your senses

Inspiring yourself

Looking after yourself

Valuing others and the world around you

Enjoying and experiencing

Re-energising and reconnecting

These six aspects overlap and intertwine, and their importance will depend on you as an individual, and where and how you are seeking inspiration. Flutter down onto the pages in any order you please.

The ideas aren't exclusively for older people, but I've written them with the older person in mind. They should suit anyone who has health difficulties, sometimes feels a little lonely, or is unsure of their place in the world and how to engage with others.

They are for anyone who doesn't recognise themselves in the mirror and can't do what they used to do; for anyone whose status has changed, or who has changes ahead that may not be entirely welcome; and for anyone who is looking for ways to engage with someone older than themselves.

These ideas are also for anyone who isn't experiencing any of those things, but wouldn't say no to having a life that is a bit happier, healthier, and easier.

Whatever frame of mind you're in, welcome to Happy Silver People!

To live is the rarest thing
in the world.
Most people just exist.

Oscar Wilde

Stimulating your senses

1. Have a super-sensory week
2. Not to be sniffed at
3. Sounds in the silence
4. Touchy and feely
5. You've got to fill a pocket or two
6. The eyes have it
7. Make way for colour
8. Very tasteful
9. Mood music
10. Halfway up the stairs

Go to the Happy Silver People website if you'd like to download task sheets for this section

1. Have a super-sensory week

As we grow older, the way our senses give us information about the world around us changes. Sight and hearing become less sharp and may fail and, after we hit sixty, our tastebuds become less able to distinguish the nuances of different flavours. Then, as we reach our seventies, our sense of smell also starts to fade, which can exacerbate our loss of taste.

So that we can continue to engage in the world around us and keep our brain cells firing, it's really important that we're proactive about exercising our senses of sight, sound, smell, taste, and touch. Naturally, our senses overlap, so you may find that by stimulating one, you are also stimulating others.

Let me introduce you to my daughter, Laura. She is a tall, slim young lady with a wide smile. I think she's beautiful but admit to being a little biased. If you spoke to her, she might sing-song "Hello"' to you, despite having a dummy (or two, or occasionally three) in her mouth, as she has the cognitive age of a toddler. A little extra material on her fifteenth chromosome has led to a rare condition with a significant impact on Laura's development and the way her senses work.

Laura has what is termed 'proprioceptive' needs. Without you even realising it, right now, your brilliant brain may be telling you that are sitting on a sofa, and whether that sofa is soft or firm, where the arms and back are, how far away the other furniture in the room is, and how you will need to position yourself to get up. But the messages that our brains send, about where we are in relation to what's around us, don't fire properly for Laura.

Exploring how she experiences the world can teach us something about what we might do to exercise our own sensory skills.

Laura is never completely still, constantly shifting and fidgeting, pushing and resisting, so as to interpret her physical environment in relation to herself. Sometimes she will cling on to you really tightly, and press her head onto yours as if she is trying to crush your skull. She also seeks stimulation through her hands by slapping and clawing, and went through a long phase of testing out door hinges with her fingers; we realised early on that her pain threshold level is high.

She also instinctively uses her mouth to experience new things, without the ability to discriminate: earth, sand, fluff, bulbs, berries, dead flies and sheep poop included. Laura has always sought out strong tastes such as marmite, curry and lemons and, to really stimulate her taste buds, she'll put toast with marmite into her mouth upside down (the toast that is, not her), so that the more flavoursome spread hits her tongue before the bread does.

Laura has a talent for picking up snippets of tunes very quickly, with a repertoire ranging from *Mary Had a Little Lamb* through *The Lonely Goatherd* to *Roar* by Katy Perry. She'll also approximate the words and sing them with a warble that would make an opera diva proud. However, too much noise or sounds at a certain pitch or volume can be very distressing or over-stimulating for her.

In terms of her vision, she'll pick out a specific single blade of grass that she must pick, in amongst a wide wildflower border in full bloom, but will pay no attention to the giraffe looming over the railings of the enclosure just behind it.

Her sense of smell is noticeably the least developed; she'll shove away anything fragrant I encourage her to sniff at and will be undeterred in her determination to handle or eat anything that utterly reeks to me.

What have I learned from my daughter's interaction with the world around her?

- That our sense of touch and spatial awareness seems to be fundamental to understanding our environment and our place in it. As we grow older we can seek out different ways to keep on physically experiencing our environment.

- That sight and sound help us to zone right in on things we choose to focus on, while filtering those of less interest. However, it's important we keep exercising these two senses so that we also have a full picture of our environment.

- That we should, if we can, nurture our closely-linked senses of taste and smell. This will help us retain the ability to enjoy the nuances of a wide range of flavours, and also enable us to unlock memories and impressions of the past.

We'll be looking at each of the senses in the next few sections, but here's a way to ease yourself in with a week of sensory activities:

Day	My Sensory Week
Masterplan Monday	I set aside some time on Monday to plan how I'm going to exercise my senses this week and set up everything I'd need...
Tasty Tuesday	When it comes to workday lunches, I tend to be a creature of habit. This is an opportunity to try something different, so I order orzo with a Mediterranean salad and grilled halloumi. I slow myself down to savour each mouthful, enjoying a new combination of tastes and textures. I'll be ordering it again soon (and I'll just sneak in a mention for the Naked Deli café in Bournemouth).
Watch out Wednesday	I retrieve from a dusty shelf one of my big, old coffee-table books. It has a blue sky cover, which captures an open-air sculpture exhibition at Chatsworth House in the Peak District. I remember how much I loved experiencing each of the giant artworks on display. I'm now looking out for a similar exhibition next year - and the book is back on view again.

Touchy Thursday	I'd planned to have a barefoot walk in the garden, but we've had a night of heavy rainfall. I venture out anyway and make cool, wet footprints in the grass. My feet feel very 'awake'!
Fragrant Friday	I pamper my hands and elbows with body lotion I was given for Christmas, now a few months ago. The juniper and burnt orange smell lovely and I breathe it in deeply, transported back to festive activities over the years.
Sounds like Saturday	This is the day to tune into an afternoon radio show which features new bands. Before too long I'm pleased to have a new favourite song to add to my own playlist. It's called *Chaise Longue* by a band from the Isle of Wight called Wet Leg. They deserve lots of airplay. (And have since had it!)
Super-Sensory Sunday – all five senses in one day!	I make myself a different breakfast with wild berries on my muesli, instead of my beloved banana, and tangy kefir added to my soya milk. It's a tasty combination to start the day, and the smell of the berries takes me back to summer. Later on, I sit for 30 minutes on my peanut ball. This gets me thinking about my balance, while also keeping me away from the temptation of touching my keyboard while I try to watch a film. I am not a huge fan of musicals and never liked Abba (that definitely wasn't my kind of music in the '70s), but I have selected *Mamma Mia* to extend my experience and, to my surprise, I find myself smiling - and even singing along a few times. I might even watch it again! What a great way to finish a super-sensory week.

Now it's your turn to set aside time over the next week to focus on each of your senses:

Day	Your Sensory Week
Masterplan Monday	
Tasty Tuesday	
Watch out Wednesday	
Touchy Thursday	
Fragrant Friday	
Sounds like Saturday	
Super-Sensory Sunday – all five senses in one day!	

2. Not to be sniffed at

Let's take a closer look at each of our senses in turn, starting with the one we possibly take most for granted - until it starts to deteriorate as we age: our sense of smell.

This deterioration not only means we generally become less aware of smells, but it impacts on our ability to discriminate *between* smells. In addition, because smell and taste are closely related, they can affect our appetite and the pleasure we get from food and drink. And, if that wasn't enough, losing this sense can weaken connections to neural pathways which help us retrieve our memories. Who knew that our noses have such an important role to play in our lives?

What happens when we breathe in a smell?

When we pick up the scent of something, for example, baking bread, what we're receiving is the odour molecules from the heated dough floating through the air. These molecules reach our nostrils and dissolve in the mucus on the ceiling of each one. Beneath this mucus is a sheath called the olfactory epithelium which contains specialized receptor cells which can detect thousands of different odours.

These receptors then transmit the odour signals to olfactory bulbs, located at the back of our noses. It's these bulbs that send odour signals to different parts of our brain like the piriform cortex, thalamus, amygdala, and hippocampus. These brain centres then go through your back catalogue of memories: the people, places, or events you associate with that smell. This helps shape what that smell is telling you, and whether you like it or not.

Just as the Star Trek transporter could beam the crew of Starship Enterprise down into a different time and place, so certain scents can whisk us off to our recollections of the past.

A whiff of salted seaweed, for example, may immediately take you back to rock-pooling as a child, bamboo fishing net in hand, balancing precariously to avoid stepping on a savagely-pointed sea-urchin. As bright sunlight bounces on the water, you're searching once again under green undulating tendrils for hermit crabs and darting sand-coloured fish; salt and sand stick to the sun cream on your warm, pink calves, while the sea rolls and sucks behind you.

Try it yourself quickly. Where would these smells transport you? What images, sensations, and feelings do they conjure up?

- lemons
- mown grass
- boiling milk
- wood smoke
- cloves

Some smells, of course, may have a personal association with something negative. If you had an awful experience working in a café, for example, you may develop a dislike for the aroma of freshly brewed coffee.

As well as the association with bad memories, another reason for an aversion to certain odours can be that nature is alerting us to danger, or that those around us have taught us that a certain smell is unpleasant to keep us from harm.

One of the worst smells ever recorded came from a substance called thioacetone. It's considered to be a dangerous chemical owing to its odour being so utterly foul that it can induce vomiting or even render people unconscious for miles around.

In 1889, thioacetone was the subject of experiments in a laboratory in Freiberg, Germany. Unfortunately, one chemical reaction produced a stink so bad that it leaked out of the building. The vile smell swept through the city, causing widespread panic and evacuation, along with a lot of people bringing up their breakfast in the street.

Otherwise, the top three smelliest things occurring in nature are...

3

At number three, it's durian, a fruit native to Southeast Asia. With its hard, spiky skin, it looks like a large green porcupine. While it tastes pretty good – a bit like caramel - and it packs some nutrients, it, unfortunately, has an appalling smell, often described as similar to rotten onions, a gas leak, or sewage. In fact, its odour can be so over-powering that it has been banned from public buildings and transport.

2

Coming in at number two is one of our furry friends, but don't be beguiled by its cute face and cuddly-looking fur. The Lesser Anteater, also known as the tamandua, emits a revolting reek from its anal glands and is seven times smellier than the infamous skunk. It lives in South and Central America, warding off unwanted visitors and predators with its stench.

1

And in the coveted number one spot is a not-so-fragrant flower known affectionately, and accurately, as the Stinking Corpse Lily. This lily has large red petals with white spots and a centre that looks like a live volcano and, at one metre across, also has the distinction of being the largest single flower in the world.

Why does it smell so putrid? It needs to attract carrion flies which are its potential pollinators. This remarkable plant is the national flower of Indonesia, but is sadly on the verge of extinction and is now a protected species. Will we see the survival of the smelliest?

There's probably little chance we'll lose so much of our sense of smell that we can't detect a lesser anteater roaming around the neighbourhood or some cellophane-wrapped corpse lilies in a bucket outside the local petrol station. However, a deterioration can cause us to enjoy life a little less, miss out on triggers for our emotions and memories, and feel detached from the world around us.

We may also not be aware of how we or our clothes or our homes smell, or perhaps over-compensate in the fear that we do.

I think now may be the perfect time to share two pieces of good news!

- ✔ Our sense of smell is typically the one that stays active for the longest
- ✔ We can counteract the decline in our sense of smell to some degree.

Our noses, it seems, are immensely trainable. Someone who fine-tuned her sense of smell to a high degree was Helen Keller, who had lost her ability to see or hear by the age of nineteen months.

Her experience was that 'the atmosphere is charged with countless odours', and she became able to distinguish different buildings she was passing, the time of day, the weather, and activities going on around her, through her refined sense of smell.

She was also able to determine one rose from another and could tell if she was standing next to an artist, a carpenter, a mason, or a chemist.

It can take years of intensive training to become an expert perfumer or sommelier, but you can improve your 'scent IQ' by practising regularly with whatever is around you.

Here are six simple ways you can start to stimulate your sense of smell, to keep it active and alert as you grow older:

Follow your nose

Take time to savour the smell of what you eat and drink. When you're about to sip your expresso, take a forkful of stir fry, or bite into a brandy snap, get up close and really relish its aroma before you consume it. I guarantee this will make it taste better, in addition to making your sense of smell that much sharper.

Linger a little longer

Studies have shown that extending your sniffing for just a bit longer can strengthen your brain's ability to process information and help you to recognise and interpret smells more efficiently. So don't hold back your nose – especially when you're in the comfort of your own home!

Stretch your smelling skills

Do you remember your olfactory bulbs which I mentioned earlier? Well, researchers at the University of Dresden's Smell and Taste Clinic found people with an average sense of smell can increase the size of these bulbs by trying out four aromas, twice a day, for about thirty seconds each.

Start by selecting four smells of which you are fond. I began with my fragrant favourites: bananas, parmesan cheese, smoky lapsang souchong tea, and Pears soap. Give yourself two minutes to smell each one individually to stimulate the receptors inside your nose, and repeat this three or four times each day for a week. Then move on to another set of four smells for each subsequent week.

Who knows, one day you may have smelling skills to rival that of a bear! Grizzlies can sniff out an elk carcass that's underwater, polar bears can catch the scent of a seal through three feet of ice, and black bears have been observed to trek eighteen miles straight to a source of food. I certainly can't match that, but I reckon I could detect a chocolate éclair in a lead-lined fridge while wearing a deep-sea diving helmet.

Protect your smell power

Vitamin B12 deficiency can lead to a partial or complete loss of smell, so make sure you get enough of this vitamin by eating fish, meat, eggs, and dairy products like cheese, milk, or yoghurt. If you're a vegan this is the most difficult vitamin to incorporate into your diet naturally. B12-fortified foods such as Marmite can be a good source if you prefer not to take supplements. Don't forget to give these foods a good sniff before eating them.

Become more 'aroma aware'

Choose an object or two to match up with these smells:

Type of smell	What might it describe?
Rancid	
Sweet	
Musty	
Pungent	
Putrid	
Acrid	
Fruity	
Metallic	
Smoky	
Minty	
Tangy	
Fresh	
Damp	
Anosmic (no smell)	

What's your reaction to each? What's the reason you feel that way?

Could you change your view?

PS If you're a smoker, you may find you can't appreciate the taste of many foods as intensely as you did before you started. Unfortunately, smoking negatively affects your sense of smell, which then also reduces your ability to taste.

Smell is a potent wizard that transports us across a thousand miles and all the years we have lived

Helen Keller

3. Sounds in the silence

Who could resist the prospect of walking deep into the Sahara, hundreds of miles from roads and habitation, where the borders of Algeria, Niger, and Mali meet? No, not me!

And so, with Tuareg guides and six Swiss strangers, I sweated my way up onto a vast high plateau to marvel at cave paintings depicting life 8,000 years ago, including, some believe, spacemen on a visit to earth.

Under the relentless sun, I could hear an occasional burst of chatter from our small group, the regular glugging of water from flasks, and frequent gasps for breath as we plodded on through the lunar landscape in the punishing heat. After nightfall, the temperature dropped unforgivingly.

Bedded down under an immense sky, thick with stars, I would sense the desert settling too: skyscraper-sized rocks cracked their joints, pebbles shifted, and sand trickled. From time to time, a solitary small creature scurried by. The remotest desert was never truly silent. If you listened.

In contrast, everyday life all too often brings with it the intrusive roar of planes overhead, ground-shaking road works, and the drone of lawnmowers on the first sunny weekend in months.

In addition, there's all the background noise that we learn to blot out: trains passing, distant traffic, the hum of appliances, clocks ticking, partners snoring.

I'm going to ask you to take some time to stretch your listening skills, and deploy them so that you are more aware of what's around you. Three tiny bones, named after the work of a blacksmith, will help you: the hammer, the anvil, and the smallest and lightest bone in your body, the stirrup.

Separating the outer ear on the side of your head from your middle ear is a thin tympanic membrane, and waves of sound cause it to vibrate. The three tiny blacksmith bones in your middle ear pick up these vibrations and transmit them towards your inner ear, into the fluid-filled hearing organ, your cochlea.

As the fluid rolls, like ocean waves, 25,000 nerve endings are set into motion, transforming the vibrations into electrical impulses that travel along the auditory nerve to your brain. Your brain then interprets these signals and you 'hear' the noise. Doesn't that sound amazing?

It's easy to exercise your ears by sitting, listening intently, and capturing a few moments in sound by drawing a map of what you hear.

Here's an example from a sunny Thursday afternoon in July in a field on the outskirts of the city of Bristol.

I am daintily seated on a warm stone resembling a giant oyster shell, encircled by five slender Scots pines. In the 1800s the land belonged to the wealthy Tuckett family, who planted a tree for each of their children around a pennant stone which marks where their favourite pony, Tom Tit, was buried.

This is also the wishing stone of my childhood, and it has heard many dreams of new bikes, boots, and boyfriends over the years.

After sharing my updated wish (to one day see Happy Silver People displayed in a bookshop window, naturally), I sat and listened.

And this is what I heard...

Sound Map
Tuckett Field, outside Bristol, UK
Thursday 8 July from 3.55 to 4.05 pm

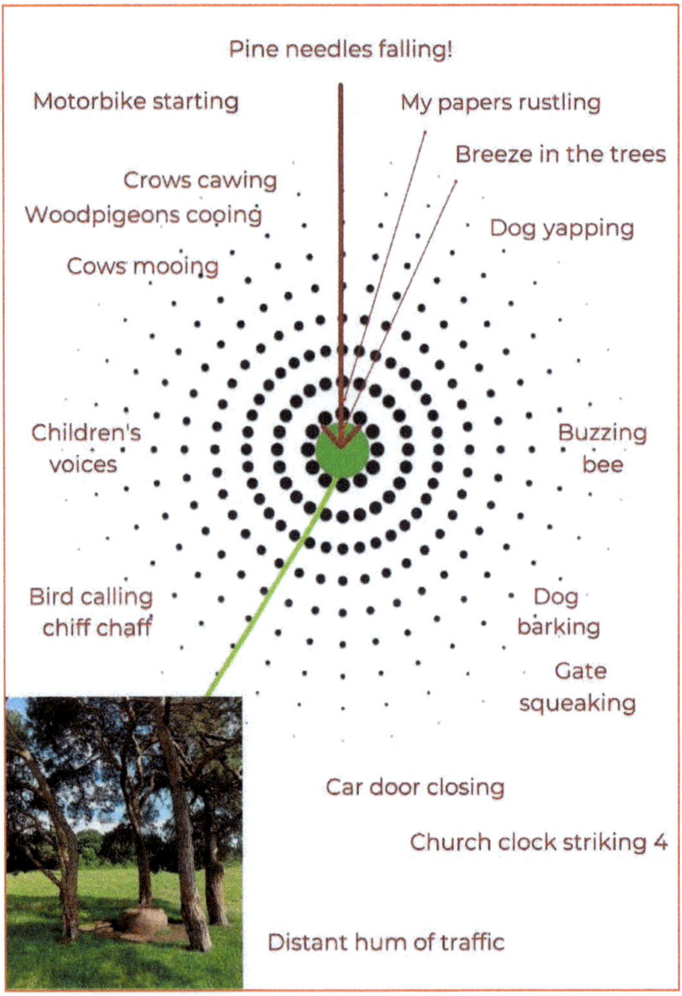

Over ten minutes I repeatedly zoned my listening out to the far reaches of what I could hear, and then came back in close again.

Top tip: As I couldn't identify all the birdsong, I downloaded the BirdNet app to my phone. I now know which feathery friend is singing out to me.

Now it's your turn to draw a sound map radiating out from where you are. You can do this indoors or outdoors. In the park, in the car, in bed. Just about anywhere you like.

Plot what you hear – the immediate sounds, what you hear beyond that, and beyond that again. Stretch your listening further and further away...

Place:

Date:

Time:

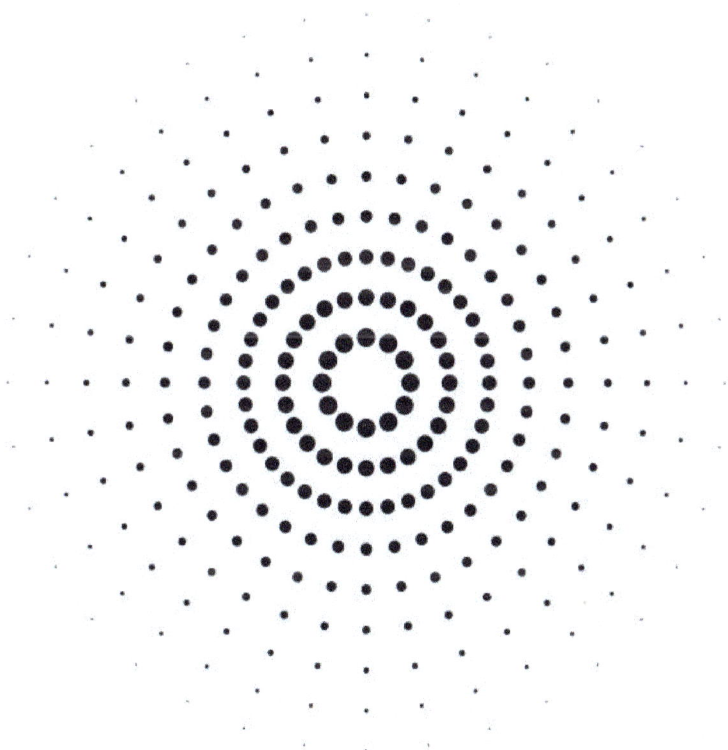

4. Touchy and feely

My guess is that you're probably reading this sitting down. If so, what are you aware of in terms of what your body is touching? Is the seat hard under your butt, with the edge maybe digging into the back of your legs a little, or it is soft and squishy?

If you're on a train or bus, your fingertips may be touching the smooth pages of this book, while your arms are uncomfortably close to your sides on account of the people next to you spilling into your space.

If indoors, you may feel the balls of your feet touching a cool wooden floor, or your heels resting on a padded footstool. Perhaps you can feel the clothes you are wearing against your skin, particularly if they are scratchy or a little too tight.

And if you're actually standing in a store while browsing through this book, please go straight to the till to pay, and carry on reading in the comfort of your own home!

Touch, the sense that most preoccupies Lovely Laura, is, for the majority of us, the one we overlook the most. Every second of every day, we receive a ton of tactile information about the world around us - so much so, that the only way we can deal with it is to tune most of it out. You probably weren't paying much attention to what you could feel, until I asked you about it.

Interestingly, our brains pay different amounts of attention to touch as it affects different parts of our bodies. This is because the part of our brain which processes touch information holds a very distorted map of our body surface.

Areas like our face, lips, tongue, and fingers have lots of fine touch receptors so they are over-represented; areas like our chest, back, and thighs are under-represented as they have far fewer.

If our bodies were re-drawn to reflect the proportion of how touch sensors are represented in the brain, we would have ginormous hands, feet, lips, and tongues, while our torsos and legs would be puny. (Search online for a 'cortical homunculus' to get a good look).

These helpful receptors come in four varieties: one to sense vibrations, one for small amounts of movement or slippage, one to sense any stretching of the skin, and one that senses the finest of textures - particularly important for your lips and fingertips.

When tactile signals become very strong, perhaps in a time of danger, or when lost in loud live music or having a relaxing massage, information coming in from our other senses - sight, sound, smell, and taste - becomes far less important.

Our sense of touch also dulls with time, but we lose our receptors very, very slowly from the age of around eighteen. On the plus side, this means we may not be as sensitive to temperature or feel as much surface pain in our skin as we grow older.

However, it may also mean that we are less aware of the warnings that touch receptors bring – that we are losing our balance, are about to burn ourselves, or need to put on an extra layer of clothing.

How can we exercise our sense of touch? I think back to Grannie Gwen in her final years when she was quite confused, couldn't see too well, and didn't talk much.

Every time my brother, James, visited, she would pull him close and tip his head forward, then rub her hand repeatedly over his shaved head. She loved the feel of it and found it hilariously funny. And now my daughter does the same.

You're going to put yourself on a 'touch diet'- and here's what's on the sensory menu:

- Put together a selection of different coins (maybe give them a good old scrub first?). With your eyes closed, run your fingers over them and see what you tell about the shape and design

- Stroke a fine paint or basting brush (ideally clean) over different parts of your face, across your shoulders and chest, down your arms and the back of your hands, across your palms, then down the back and front of your legs, and along the top and soles of your feet.

  Can you feel how various parts of your body respond to the same stimulus in different ways?

- Create a touch toolbox with a variety of textures to explore. For example, fir cones, sandpaper, cotton wool, bubble wrap, walnuts, snail shells and foil, plus scraps of different fabrics such as wool, corduroy, leather, canvas, silk, faux fur, sequins, tassels, netting, satin and lace.

- Do some barefoot walking, in the house, in the garden, on the beach, wherever you can

- Take a moment at different times of the day to focus on what your body can physically feel – what's beneath your feet, the clothes you are wearing, the wind or rain on your face, your fingers touching your mouse or keyboard or steering wheel, the handle of a cup in your hand, your back against the seat, your cheek against your pillow.

Make sure you don't miss out on touch as a way of experiencing your world!

5. You've got to fill a pocket or two

I know how it feels to suffer from anxiety: stomach-churching, nervous-making, heart-pumping, overpowering, breath-taking, butt-clenching, fun-draining, sad-living, stress-giving, cold-sweating anxiety.

Growing up. I could be painfully shy and hated being singled out. Many times, the number 326 green double-decker bus bringing me home from school, would sail on past where I should have got off. I refused to draw attention to myself by standing up to press the bell for it to stop.

It may sound strange that I started to address my social anxiety by wearing outlandish outfits. I figured that if people were going to look at me, it would be because of my clothes not anything intrinsic about me.

This led to various outfits featuring: a plastic parrot sitting on my left shoulder; a pair of antique leopard-skin spats; black mediaeval-style breeches; original and somewhat uncomfortable winkle pickers with steel-capped heels; an over-sized, rather hairy Mexican poncho; a midnight-blue tabard; binbag dresses; my dad's green silk dressing down; and the faded striped PJs of a friend's father who was a foot taller than me.

Because I chose my wardrobe, I felt I could determine how much attention I got. And sometimes it was an awful lot: passing cars would weave, and cyclists would wobble.

Growing up, I didn't know what I wanted to do in life. My only certainty was that I never wanted to become a teacher. But educating others was a way for me to pursue my passion for travel and I found I not only enjoyed supporting adults and children with their learning but, to my surprise, was quite good at it. Standing up in front of groups of strangers helped me become more genuinely confident.

At first, I found security through thorough planning and preparation, and then, in time, I started to know and share my 'stuff'. This is still true for me today: I could speak to a cathedral full of several hundred people at my father's memorial service because I had been able to practise beforehand, and nowadays talking into a TV camera on a familiar topic is not so daunting. However, job interviews, meeting new people, and some social events remain butterfly-makers, and my secret weapon on these occasions is a pocket pebble secreted about my person.

Now, obviously, the ideal place for a pocket pebble is in a handy pocket. Surely, there is something fundamentally amiss with skirts or trousers which are deficient in the pocket department? But these day-to-day essentials are a surprisingly recent feature of our clothing, especially for we lasses (and for wee lassies too).

The word 'pocket' comes from 'poque', an old northern French word for a bag, which came to mean a small pouch attached to, or inserted into, a garment. The Iceman, a naturally persevered mummy of a man who lived around 3200 BCE, was discovered in the Ötztal Alps on the border between Austria and Italy, and had such a pouch strapped to his belt, holding some of his valuable items (possibly including a pebble).

But while pockets first started appearing on waistcoats and trousers for chaps around 500 years ago, chap-esses still tied on a separate pouch between the skirt and petticoat they were wearing that day, keeping a multiplicity of treasures safely hidden: pencils and pincushions; coins and combs; thimbles and toothpicks; keys and cherry cake.

That is, until the fashion of late Victorian times brought an end to the wonderfully practical pouch. With new slimmer skirts and a striving for weeny waists, pouches couldn't be hidden away anymore. Instead, women attached 'reticules' to the outside of their dresses, and the daintier the better, as this indicated a life of leisure and a husband and servants who oversaw all practical matters.

And this explains how the rather careless Lucy Locket was able to lose her 'pocket', and how eagle-eyed Kitty Fisher could find it.

There was a proper pocket comeback after the turn of the twentieth century when women also started wearing the trousers and the needs of wartime led to a more practical approach to clothing, but this was snatched away once again with slimmer silhouettes and the birth of the handbag.

Pockets were shunned by stylists, with the new approach summed up by Christian Dior in 1954, "Men have pockets to keep things in, women for decoration."

A huge hoorah then for the phenomenon of Levi jeans, with a place for everything: your coins, bus ticket, wallet, comb, and lippy - plus a small, special legacy space front right, if you still fancy carrying a pocket watch.

You could try to emulate the multi-talented Alanis Morissette, by putting one hand in your pocket while using the other to give a high five, flick a cigarette, give a peace sign, play the piano, and hail a taxicab – all within the time it takes to strum a song.

Let's celebrate our modern-day pockets, by popping in a pebble. A pebble that's smooth and cool to the touch, and that you can run your fingers over in a kind of mini-meditation.

My pearly pebbles are in the Happy Silver People colours of yellow and silver grey. They are my confidence strengtheners, my memory prompts, and my smile boosters. They can also be sent to someone going through a tough time, so they know I'm thinking of them.

I have one extra-precious 'pebble'. An iridescent, glass cone which mysteriously appeared on the pavement, just outside the gate to my parents' cottage on the morning after my father had died there.

I like to think it was a gift from him, with the message: keep this in your pocket and know that I am with you; keep this in your pocket for when you need to know just how much you are loved by me.

- What could you use as a pocket pebble?
- How could you use it?
- Is there someone you could send a pocket pebble to, so they know you are thinking of them?

6. The eyes have it

I was something of a disruptive influence at school for a time when I was twelve or thirteen. Usually well-behaved, I was regularly being pulled up for talking in class, and then in a practical physics exam too (something to do with corks bobbing about in water).

Inevitably the annual appointment with the school nurse came round, attended also by my mum who was invited to sit on one of those baggy canvas chairs with a cold metal frame and hold her coat on her lap.

Having had my knees tapped and ears peered into, the moment I'd dreaded finally arrived.

"Can you read the bottom line of the letters on the chart, please?"

It was a casual question, posed rhetorically as the nurse was pretty confident about the answer I was going to give. She'd already turned away to pick up the spatula she needed to squash down my tongue and contemplate the dangly bit at the back of my throat.

My mum's unconcerned expression didn't waver during the silent pause before the nurse said, "How about the line above, then?"

The silence then resumed. I now had their full attention.

"Which letters *can* you read, Rachel?"

I had finally been rumbled. Not one of those letters was clear.

And so, my time as a spectacles-wearer began. The lenses were thick, and I felt as glamorous as Olive in *On The Buses*.

For the sake of my appearance, I took my glasses off whenever I could but, oh, when I put them back on, the world looked wonderful!

Instead of being enveloped in a blur, I could see flowers, faces, and the finest of details; colours were brighter, sharper, and richer; the writing on the blackboard and the labels on the drawers of equipment in the physics lab were clear once more, and I no longer needed to keep bothering my classmates for help. It was a relief that my increasingly desperate strategies to conceal my deteriorating eyesight were now redundant.

Fortunately, by the time I was fifteen, something called the contact lens was becoming more common in the UK and, to my joy, I was able to get a pair of hard lenses.

My parents positioned an upright chair with a small table holding a magnifying mirror in my bedroom which, as it was the 1970s, had a sink with gold taps and a sparkly Formica surround.

This was a clean, safe place for the daily routine of putting my lenses in when I woke up and then taking them out before bed, placing them in their little disinfected case to have a long soak in special, freshly-poured liquid.

As I morphed into a student, of course, a bit of spit and a quick polish on my cuff often had to suffice after sleeping in someone's bath after a party, or in a chilly photo booth after missing the last train home.

Over the years, life got progressively better with semi-permeable lenses, soft daily disposables, and varifocals, until there came the long-awaited day of laser surgery. I could now see during my every waking moment! I could see when I needed the loo in the middle of the night! Even my dreams were more in focus!

I now have glasses once again: some for reading and, recently, others with an 'occupational prescription' which makes it much more comfortable to switch from close work to looking at a screen and back again.

But the choice of frames now is phenomenal. It's time to say au revoir to Olive and to emulate Elton instead.

Like me, you may well be noticing changes in your vision as you grow older. As we age, we can expect to experience:

- being less able to see up close (aka needing to have much, much longer arms)
- difficulty distinguishing colours, such as black and blue (but who says your socks have to match?)
- needing more time to adjust to variations in lighting levels.

These normal alterations in the ageing eye usually don't harm vision: glasses, contact lenses, and improved lighting may all help. However, be mindful that sometimes these changes, or sudden blurry or double vision, eye pain, flashes of light or lots of 'floaters', can be signs of something more serious.

When it comes to your eyes, please don't play the ostrich as I once did! Our risk of developing certain eye diseases and conditions increases as we grow older, and we may not notice any signs or symptoms in the early stages.

A dilated eye exam every year is recommended for everyone aged over fifty, even if you (think you) have good vision and don't wear contacts or glasses. If you do wear them, get your prescription checked regularly, too.

Small changes in your sight can increase your risk of accidents, falls, and injuries - and remember to take your time adjusting to a new prescription. My father spectacularly descended a ladder from top to bottom in just one step, after ill-advisedly going up to look for elf ears in the roof of the garage, while wearing his brand-new bifocals.

The potentially more serious eye problems which an optometrist or an ophthalmologist will look out for include: age-related macular degeneration (AMD) which can harm the sharp, central vision you need to see objects clearly and to do everyday activities such as driving and reading; cataracts which are cloudy areas in the lens of the eye causing blurred or hazy vision; and glaucoma which often causes no early symptoms or pain but can lead to vision loss if left untreated.

Dry eye can also be a common complaint as people get older, especially women. It occurs when your tear glands don't work well, leading to a stinging, burning, or scratchy feeling as if something is in your eye. Measures such as special eye drops (artificial tears) or using an air purifier can help to treat this condition.

Here are seven things you can start doing today to take good care of your eyes and help keep them healthy as you age:

- ✔ Make regular appointments to get your eyes and prescriptions checked
- ✔ Shield your eyes from sunlight by wearing protective sunglasses. Consider wrap-around shades, as the side of the face can be quite vulnerable to cancerous growths
- ✔ Make eye-smart food choices such as carrots, red berries, red and green papers, plus kiwi fruit, broccoli and spinach which are all great sources of vitamin A. Add onions too, as the selenium they contain can help your body to produce eye-friendly vitamin E
- ✔ If you spend a lot of time at the computer or focusing your gaze on one thing, try the 20:20:20 approach - take a break every 20 minutes to look about 20 feet away for 20 seconds, and make a conscious effort to blink frequently
- ✔ Consider carefully whether you have sufficient natural or artificial lighting for different tasks during the day
- ✔ If you are taking a little longer to adjust to changes in lighting levels, think about using motion lighting both indoors and out

- Use plug-in night lights which are automatically activated when it starts getting dark to give yourself a little extra illumination along hallways, on landings, and in other darker corners

- Relax your eyes regularly with a cool eye mask that you can keep in the fridge, or one you can warm in the microwave or with boiling water

- Take a long-range approach to managing your blood pressure levels, reducing the risk or impact of diabetes, and cutting down on smoking to decrease your chance of developing an eye condition.

It never hurts
your eyesight
to look on the
bright side of things

Barbara Johnson

7. Make way for colour

A few years ago, I overheard two people chatting in a sitting room:

"I've ordered some new cushions for this sofa," said my friend
"How nice!" said her sister-in-law. "What colour are they?"
"Well, the website described them as 'toffee'."
"So, what kind of colour is that then?" asked the sister-in-law
"Ummm. I'm not exactly sure. Toffee-coloured, I think"
"Oooooh! How lovely!" her sister-in-law cooed.

In hindsight, maybe it wasn't as ridiculous a conversation as I thought at the time. There's treacle toffee, cinder toffee, Brazil nut toffee, and caramel toffee – all with scrumptiously different hues of toffee-ness.

Thinking more broadly about beautiful browns, my friend could have selected cushions that were almond, coffee, mahogany, oatmeal, taupe, umber, walnut, or prune.

We all know by now that there are 50+ shades of grey. For starters, I can think of lead, anthracite, and slate; nimbostratus, drizzle, and puddle; pigeon, squirrel, and vole; cannonball, paving slab, and manhole cover. What am I missing?

How about the palette opposite? What would these shades be called if you owned the paint factory?

	Name of colour
A	
B	
C	
D	
E	
F	
G	

My thoughts were: damp brickwork, peppermint cream, match day cancelled, throw the curtains wide, borscht, golden dahl, and camel hoof.

We're aware that colours can affect our moods: reds and oranges are often used in fast food outlets to encourage us to eat more quickly and move on, while spas and health centres use blues to evoke the restful waves of the ocean.

Colour psychologists also suspect that the colour of the vehicle you choose may say something about you: white is associated with youth and modernity; black, the most popular colour for luxury cars, is seen as powerful; silver, the third most popular colour is linked to innovation and modernity; red is bold and attention-grabbing, and so may project an image of action and confidence; blue is seen as representing stability, safety and dependability; driving a yellow vehicle might mean that you are generally a happy person, and may be more of a risk-taker; while drivers of grey cars perhaps don't want to stand out, preferring something more subtle.

More scientific research is needed to gain a better understanding of colour psychology; while colour does seem to influence how we feel and act, these effects are subject to personal, cultural, and situational factors.

The impact of colour upon us may also change, of course, as we grow older and suddenly different colours attract us and impact our mood in new ways.

It's time to take a fresh look at the impact colours have on you:

Which make you feel:

- ? calm and relaxed?
- ? energised and motivated?
- ? confident and ready to take on the world?

On the next page, draw lines to link the emotions to the different shades you associate with them.

Feel free to add more emotions if you wish...

Confident
Fearful
Energised
Cross
Calm
Happy
Sad
Relaxed
Dispirited
Hopeful

Consider which colours influence your personal sense of well-being. Be intentional about the colours you bring into your world and your wardrobe.

Last year, I wanted to inject more yellow, as a happy colour, into my life. In my working space, pineapple-coloured walls would probably have been a bit distracting so, instead, I bought a door stop (with pompoms), picture frames, plant pots, a clock, and a rug in complementary honeyed shades.

In terms of clothing, sunshine yellow can make my skin look like uncooked pastry, but other shades, as an accent, work well to boost my mood.

I am now the proud owner of a dandelion-coloured sales-bargain jacket, a striped jumper in more muted mustardy shades, and a zingy geometric scarf.

I can also confidently advise that yellow tights are a complete no-no. Unless you have the shapeliest of knees or are appearing in panto.

> I prefer living life in colour
>
> David Hockney

8. Very tasteful

It's not a happy pill to swallow, but let's not sugar-coat it. Although we're born with around 10,000 taste buds, between the ages of forty and fifty, their number will be decreasing, and the remaining ones will start shrinking, meaning they are less effective. So, from the age of sixty, we may be less able to distinguish sweet, salty, sour, savoury, and bitter flavours and, as we touched on earlier, this fading sense of smell can also impact on our sense of taste.

On the plus side, these changes may mean we're able to tolerate a wider range of tastes as we grow older. 'Grown-up' foods such as broccoli or olives which we hated when younger, now seem to taste delicious - we may even select different favourites depending on our mood: purple-sprouting or tenderstem; kalamata or manzanilla.

In the past few years, I've been a zealous convert to Marmite but must confess I still can't get myself to like carrots. My parents were ever-hopeful that I would somehow 'learn to like them', as I was banished to the playroom to munch my way through yet another orange-coloured mound in solitude.

Fortunately, there was a window that opened, and I could just reach the latch on tiptoes. One by one, the slices of carrot would fly from my fork, arcing gracefully through the air, before nose-diving into the flower border below. Mum and Dad would be delighted at the sight of my empty plate, I was rewarded with a couple of scoops of raspberry ripple ice cream, and the roses thrived.

Now let's explore those five types of taste a bit further:

Salty

We're aware of the negatives associated with too much salt, but it plays an important part in our diet and the relationship we have with our food. Salt has a role as a flavour enhancer, bringing out the sweetness and blocking any bitterness, and the right mix of these different taste elements triggers a positive response in our brains.

This is why salty foods can work well in seemingly strange combinations. Think bacon and pancakes with golden syrup; Stilton and pears or Manchego and quince jelly; salty caramel-covered almonds; roast pork and apple sauce; sea salt and olive oil with vanilla ice cream; cottage cheese with fruit cake; or mackerel and banana sandwiches. I acknowledge the last one, in particular, may be an acquired taste.

While our palates can adapt to crave more and more salt in our diet, our taste buds can also adjust to much less. Salt can be replaced in home cooking with an imaginative use of a range of herbs and spices, including more pepper, but if you're seeking a snack with a smidgeon of saltiness, my recommendation is gentleman's anchovy relish, Patum Peperium, on hot toast with lashings of butter.

Sour

Researchers are still not completely sure about the mechanism which underlies how our sour taste receptors work or why some acids lead to a sourer flavour than others.

As with bitterness, though, detecting sourness is believed to be important for survival, as food that has gone off often has a sour flavour due to the growth of bacteria.

Of course, this doesn't mean that all sour foods are unsafe to eat. Many are quite nutritious and rich in antioxidants, which help protect our cells from damage. Sour foods also make the mouth moist and increase the flow of saliva, both of which help digestion and pleasant anticipation of our dinner on the table.

High on the list of lip-puckering foods are fruits from the citrus family, rhubarb, Chinese and Japanese plums, tamarind, kimchi, and natural yoghurt, to be washed down with fermented drinks, such as kombucha and kefir.

Sweet

As well as throwing out your salt cellar, can you gradually remove refined sugar from your home and use natural equivalents? Shift to other sources of sugars such as fresh or dried fruit, dairy products, or honey, and supplement with sugar substitutes if you need to. It may be tough at first, but gradually your taste buds will start to adjust and within a month you should notice a considerable difference. Reducing your sugar intake can not only strengthen your immune system but also lessen your risk of chronic inflammation, so increasing your body's ability to fight infections, such as colds and flu.

Savoury

A savoury flavour is also known as umami, which is Japanese for 'essence of deliciousness'. Umami compounds are often found in high-protein foods, so tasting umami tells your body that a food contains protein. In response, it secretes saliva and juices which will help your digestion.

In addition, umami-rich foods and drinks can be more filling, so choosing them may curb your appetite and help you lose weight. Examples include meat, aged cheeses, soy-based products such as tofu and miso, green tea, and the diverse and delicious range of seaweeds and mushrooms.

Bitter

A bitter taste can sometimes be a warning that a particular food is toxic; maybe it's a plant's self-protection mechanism - if you taste nasty, nothing will want to eat you! But the bitter foods and drinks we can enjoy are rich in healthy antioxidants (they're what accounts for the flavour), so it's well worth training our taste buds to appreciate them more.

If you're seeking out bitterness, go for green leafy vegetables including spinach, broccoli, cabbage, sprouts and rocket, aubergines, spices such as turmeric and fenugreek, tea and coffee, dark chocolate, ginger, grapefruits and olives, plus citrus peel.

The Queen of The Greens, however, is nutrient-loaded kale. If you massage it (yes, you read that right) for a couple of minutes before cooking, with a little oil and lemon juice, it'll become more tender. Try it shredded and crispy: sauteed kale is quick and easy and brings out more subtle flavours, rather than blanket bitterness.

And here's where you experience these five tastes on your tongue, which by the way, is one of the few parts of your body which continues to grow as you age...

As well as giving your taste buds a workout with different flavours, there are a couple of other things you can do to improve your sense of taste.

One is to swill water around your mouth before eating to give your taste buds a better chance of differentiating the flavours in your meal.

The second is to practise good dental hygiene to keep your mouth and tongue fresh, healthy, and working well.

Oh, and if you're a smoker, you could have an enhanced sense of taste within a couple of days after quitting.

It's time for you to make those taste buds tingle!

This week, for each type of taste:

- ✔ try a food you used to dislike or
- ✔ sample something new or
- ✔ experiment with a complementary combination

	What you're going to taste
Salty	
Sour	
Sweet	
Savoury or umami	
Bitter	

9. Mood music

Each of us turns to music to influence our mood in different ways. My mum, 85¾, enjoys listening to choral music, brass bands, and reggae, with the last one on the list being added in recent years.

In 2020, Dr. Jacob Jolij, a researcher in cognitive neuroscience, identified the top ten (English) songs for making us happy. He based this on examples from the public of their favourite feel-good tracks, from which he identified patterns which revealed the characteristics of songs which make us smile.

He discovered that the happiest tunes have a slightly faster beat than the average song, are written in a major key, and have uplifting content. Making the list were:

- *Don't Stop Me Now* by Queen
- *Dancing Queen* by Abba
- *Good Vibrations* by The Beach Boys
- *Uptown Girl* by Billy Joel
- *Eye of the Tiger* by Survivor
- *I'm a Believer* by The Monkees.
- *Girls Just Wanna Have Fun* by Cyndi Lauper
- *Livin' on a Prayer* by Bon Jovi
- *I Will Survive* by Gloria Gaynor
- *Walking on Sunshine* by Katrina and The Waves

I'm not sure what this says about me, but just one of these *might* make my list of 10 Happy-Time Tunes, and more than half are not going to be featuring in my top 100.

As with the influence of colour on our mood, the music we choose is affected by factors such as our background and experience.

Age may also play a part - as our sense of sound becomes less sharp, we may respond in a new way to certain pitches and tones.

Let's experiment with your responses to diverse kinds of music.

You'll need to find the ten tracks listed below on the Internet – and please listen **without** watching the videos!

A	Corinne Bailey Rae: Put Your Records On
B	Liam Gallagher's High Flying Birds: Holy Mountain
C	Górecki: Symphony No. 3, Movement No. 2
D	Amr Diab: Nour El Ein
E	CeeLo Green: Bright Lights Bigger City
F	Wet Leg: Chaise Longue
G	Tony Bennett: The Good Life (Harry R's choice)
H	Yiruma: River Flows In You
I	Bat For Lashes: Laura
J	Johnny Nash: I Can See Clearly Now

Listen to each till the end (or hang in there for a minimum of two minutes if it's really not your thing).

Think about:

- ? How is this music making me feel?
- ? What physical response do I have to it?
- ? Which colour shades would I associate with it?

Listen again with your eyes closed and consider the senses that each piece of music evokes:

- ? What do you 'see'?
- ? What can you smell, taste, and feel?
- ? How does it affect your mood?

Now consider:

- ? Which of these pieces of music might you listen to again?

Which genres of music might you explore further?

> **Life seems to go on without effort when I am filled with music**
>
> ♫
>
> George Elliot

10. Halfway up the stairs

Our house is spread over three floors: ground floor, first floor and attic, where a couple of servants once slept (with chamber pots under the bed presumably), and I now write.

I wondered which point in the house was halfway up and halfway down, and discovered it was at stair number 17, just below the first floor.

After taming the urge to burst into song, just like a little green frog, I decided to sit halfway up my stairs for a while and experience my home in a different way...

listening to the creaks and slow sighs specific to that space,
watching light filter at a new angle through the landing window,
feeling carpet, tufty beneath my palms, and the air flow around my face,
catching bird's-eye glimpses down through the bannisters and, above my head,
observing the smooth sloping underside of the staircase on its final upward stretch

I remembered playing on the stairs of my childhood home with dolls and slinkies. Later, I'd settle down for hours in my preferred spot, just below the landing, absorbed in my books or pondering the mysteries of life as revealed by Jackie magazine.

At Christmas, there were glass baubles in jewel colours hanging between each bannister, all of which I named. There was Victoria, Florence, Stephanie, Phoebe, Francesca, Miranda, Charlotte – you get the gist.

My favourite hanging ornament was deep purple, shaped like the onion-domed roof of an Eastern Orthodox church, and called Amelia. Long after she shattered into a thousand tiny slivers, her memory strangely lives on: Amelia is now one of Laura's middle names.

I've started hanging out on the stairs once again, to read or think or pause for a moment; to take the mini-est of breaks.

Is there somewhere in your home where you could sit and find a new perspective?

If you have no stairs, perhaps try the other end of the sofa, a different chair, a new corner, or a space in the garden where you wouldn't normally linger.

When you go out, try varying your usual route, sitting in another seat on the bus or train, parking in a new spot, choosing a different table in your favourite café, or taking a rest on an alternative bench.

Look for ways to experience the familiar in a fresh way. You may enjoy new sights, sounds and smells, find that you have rekindled memories of the past, or spot spiders' webs and dusty ledges you didn't know you had.

Sometimes a little change can be as good as a little rest.

> True life is lived
>
> when tiny changes occur
>
> Leo Tolstoy

Inspiring yourself

1. Charged with creativity
2. What's in a name?
3. A journal a day
4. Essence of you
5. Least said...
6. Wordilicious
7. Heavenly 17
8. Making an exhibition for yourself
9. Poetry in motion
10. Named and framed

Go to the Happy Silver People website if you'd like to download task sheets for this section

1. Charged with creativity

Crowds jostle in the courtroom. Cameras flash and pop. In the over-stuffed public gallery, necks are craned as everyone attempts to glimpse me. In a staid skirt and sensible shoes, I wipe perspiration from my brow, while the scraggy-necked judge, resplendent in weighty black robes and a tightly-rolled wig towers over me.

“And just how do you plead to the charge of not being creative?” he asks.

“Not being creative? I would have to plead ever so guilty, my Lord,” I squeak.

“Guilty?’ He bends his head to hide a creeping smile. Then, with a hint of regret, says, “I’m afraid we will need a little evidence.”

My evidence? Hmmm. Let me think.

“Well, I failed my Art ‘O’ Level - although I was rather proud of my still-life of satsuma segments and the smudgy charcoal sketch of a tumble-down shed, complete with an array of nameless, rusty farm implements.

“At school, I knitted and sewed garments without shape, including what could have been a rather fetching purple smock. I cross-stitched a placemat, the crisp white calico gradually greying as it was passed repeatedly through my grubby fingers. Yes, I do know what a running stitch is and how to use bias binding. But only in theory.

“I can also recall hammering at wonky picture frames in woodwork, and moulding uncooperative clay into lumpy receptacles which were kindly placed in the kiln by Mr. Walters, the pottery teacher (affectionately known as Mr. Potters, the watery teacher).

“Yes, I did reach the dizzy heights of Grade 1 in Pianoforte. However, I would add in mitigation that my Saturday morning teacher, massaging her temples, would often whisper an apology for cutting short my lesson. I also passed Grade 4 for the Descant Recorder (that's the short, squeaky one), was quite proficient at *Pease Pudding Hot*, and could even manage the F-sharp in *We Three Kings*, but I was never going to charm any rodents out of the drainpipes with my tootling.

"And while it's true I could also distinguish a semi-quaver from a semi-breve, allegro from adagio, and pianissississimo from plonking my phalanges down on the piano keys as hard as I possibly could, would anyone have voluntarily listened to me play an instrument? No, no, no, my Lord. They would not.

In summary, I fear that I am, quite clearly, not creative. I rest my case and confirm my plea: I am guilty as charged."

There is a fleeting sparkle in the judge's eye as he straightens his wig, preens in his robes, and arranges his face back into a sombre expression. As the crowd hushes, he opens his mouth to proclaim my conviction.

But confident footsteps break the silence. A friend, smartly suited, eases himself into the witness stand and stages a pause before addressing the attentive throng.

"This, my Lord, is one of the most creative people I know."

The assembly straightens up. There is some ooohing and aaahing – although I can't help but notice a few dubious expressions. Indeed, I have one of my own.

"Why do I say this?" he continues.

Along with everyone else, I wonder what on earth is coming next.

"Well, there are her suggestions for change and innovation, her problem-solving skills, and her ideas for enhancing what we offer to our customers".

He goes on at embarrassing length, throwing in an assortment of examples to back up his case. Is he really talking about me? Surely this stuff doesn't count as being creative, Or does it?

Then I see the crowd. They're nodding at each other, and a few of them even let out whoops and whistles. A tentative smile escapes me.

At last, the judge croaks "Not guilty!" and, after slamming down his gavel, swoops off to look for fresh prey.

It took me many, many years to realise that creativity comes in many, many shapes and sizes, and it wasn't until I was in my fifties that anyone used the word 'creative' to describe me. In my case, the key was finding opportunities where I could shape change, or work with others to create something new.

I now know that you don't need to be able to draw or be musical to be creative. But, one day soon, I'll try drawing again - and again, and again - until my still-life of satsuma segments really sings!

You're in the courtroom now!

On a scale of 1 (min) to 5 (max), rate your creativity:

1 2 3 4 5

- ? What's the evidence for and against your score?
- ? What could you do next to enhance your rating?
- ? Which aspects of your creativity are a bit rusty and could be revived?
- ? What could you do next to move your creativity in a direction you haven't explored yet?
- ? What would be the benefits to you at this stage in your life?

2. What's in a name?

My name is Rachel.

How many times in my life have I said and written my name?

When I write it in the Roman alphabet it has six letters: four consonants and two vowels. The letter values add up to 11 in Scrabble.

I can write it forwards, backwards, vertically, or horizontally, in a spiral, circle or wave; I can mirror-write it too.

My name is originally Semitic. In Hebrew and Arabic, it's written from right to left, with three consonants plus some diacritical marks (dots and dashes) for the vowels, as רָחֵל and رَاحِيْل

Rachel exists as a name in Greek too, as Ῥαχήλ (written from left to right).

In some languages and other means of communication, my name doesn't exist as such, On the next page, you can read a representation of Rachel in Braille, Hindi, Japanese, Korean, Mandarin, Morse Code, Russian, Sign Language, and Thai.

Each image of 'Rachel' seems to convey something different. Sometimes my name looks soft and almost musical; other times, it's harder and almost brutal.

I am excited to be able to read at least one word in languages I will probably never learn. It's a way to get the tiniest insight into forms of communication that are so different from my own.

⠠⠗⠁⠉⠓⠑⠇

राहेल

麗千恵瑠

레이첼

蕾切尔

.-. .- -.-. .... . .-..

Рахиль

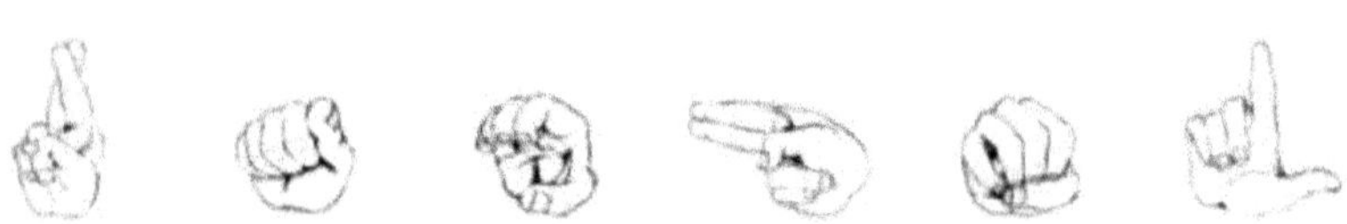

ราเชล

My name is a label attached to me, chosen for me before I was born, and intended to last a lifetime.

Did I look like a 'Rachel' as a new-born baby? What does a Rachel look like? I'm told I was almost a Rebecca or a Helen and could have been a Robert or an Andrew. My mum says that if she named a baby now, she would go for Hamish, Rowan, or Olivia.

The choice of my name was rooted in the meaning. My parents wanted a Biblical name and Rachel conveys the sense of 'much loved'.

Well, yes, technically it does mean a female sheep. Not quite so lovable as a fluffy bunny or saucer-eyed kitten you might think, but ewes were very prized in Old Testament times, and so was beautiful leading lady, Rachel. The patriarch Jacob was mesmerised by her and worked seven hard years for her father, Laban, to secure her hand in marriage.

But wily Laban tricked him and married him off to his older daughter Leah instead, without Jacob realising; wedding veils were presumably not flimsy affairs in those days. Jacob then toiled another seven years, so he could finally marry Rachel.

Jacob fathered the twelve tribes of Israel, with Rachel being the mother of the youngest two, Joseph and Benjamin. Far, far away I hear Jason Donovan still singing about that coat of many colours, given to Joseph as his father's favourite son.

I was not unhappy with my name growing up but sometimes wished for something a little more sophisticated, with a hint of mystery. I played with variations of my name such as Rachelle or Raquel, while imagining life as a Hélène (accents essential, naturally) or Celeste, or maybe even a Carlotta, Yseult, or Ophelia.

Another Name Day falls in April and represents an unexpected opportunity to try out a new name for a day.

Next time, I'm choosing to be called Zenobia. She was the courageous queen of the ancient desert city of Palmyra in Syria.

In the third century CE, she conquered Egypt, captured Roman provinces, and almost created a realm to rival that of the Roman Empire after her husband's death.

She's believed to have been a cultured leader who was tolerant towards her subjects and encouraged an intellectual environment in her court. She welcomed scholars and philosophers and protected religious minorities.

However, in 272 Zenobia reacted to the war campaign of Roman Emperor Aurelian by declaring her son Emperor of their own lands.

The Romans were savage in their response, besieging the queen in Palmyra before capturing her. Having undergone the humiliation of being paraded in golden chains during Aurelian's celebrations of triumph in Rome, her life was spared.

Aurelian was impressed by her, and she remained there in exile with her son, becoming a prominent philosopher and socialite, and possibly also marrying a nobleman or Roman senator.

I have a small painting of Zenobia on my bedroom wall. She is sitting at a window with a lute by her side, gazing out to sea. I imagine her dreaming of camels and conquests, and life as a desert queen.

For a future Another Name Day, I may create a completely new name for myself: Querca, like a mighty oak tree; Azure, reflecting the bluest of seas; Sparrow, after the little bird that is full of surprises; or Dandelion for the irrepressible, happy yellow flower who turns into the most delicate silvery sphere in the passing of time, and is then scattered in the breath of the wind.

It's time to explore your name

- What does it mean? What's the origin?
- Do you know why it was chosen for you?
- What does your name say about you? Has it said different things at different times of your life? What will it say about you in the next stage of your life?
- Would it have made a difference if you'd been called something else?
- Write your name in different ways – forwards, backwards, lowercase and capitals, vertically, and in a circle. Which do you like the look of most?
- How does your name look in languages with different scripts? How about in Braille and Sign Language, Morse code, and maybe semaphore?

The next Another Name Day comes around on 9 April

- Which name are you going to adopt for 24 hours? Why?

> Today you are you.
> That is truer than true.
> **There is no one alive**
> **Who is youer than you.**
>
> Dr Seuss

3. A journal a day

As you've probably heard by now, journaling is good for our mental health. It can be relaxing and reflective; it can help us capture our emotions, or let them go; it can remind us of the good times, and be a record of our achievements, big and small; it can help us plan the future and be positive about what lies ahead; it can encourage us to reconnect, rebuild, and put things right.

The simple old-fashioned way to do that is by keeping a diary, and Grannie Gwen was a great diarist. When she became a widow in her late sixties, my father suggested she could start keeping a diary. For the next thirty years, she noted down her daily life in a Dairy Diary – a misspelling just waiting to happen.

Each week was allotted a double page, accompanied by a photo of a culinary delicacy with the tasty recipe underneath. Standout examples included kipper pate, roast chicken with cheese and peanut stuffing, kidney stroganoff, sardine tart, and a boozy marshmallow flan. Thank heavens she was never tempted to make any of these and try them out on us.

Each of her diary entries starts with the weather: a drizzly morning mist perhaps, or a sweltering afternoon before thunderstorms.

And then there were the day's activities. Regular callers over the years included the Kleen-eze man with an array of tempting tea towels and dusters, well-meaning Maurice from next door, and the TV technician from Radio Rentals.

There were plentiful meetings at the WI, Friendly Circle, and Ladies' Club to be enjoyed, as well as trips to church, and times with the family. There was vacuuming, washing, and window cleaning to be done, plus the waste disposal to be cleaned out. The bank, the dentist, and the doctor were visited; letters were sent and received; and strawberries, raspberries, and gooseberries were all picked. Batteries were bought for the clock and the doorbell; endless china cups of tea were consumed; scones and slices of Victoria sponge were savoured. In between, Grannie Gwen's hair was shampooed and set, and occasionally permed by Janet.

And once, Songs of Praise was broadcast from Llandudno.

Grannie Gwen didn't refer much to world events or include personal reflections, feelings, or thoughts at all.

What did she get out of her diarising? I'm guessing that reading back through the entries she'd made, she felt that life was still going on, she had new happy memories, and things she could still look forward to.

She certainly lived her many years of widowhood as fully as she could, and it seems that recording just a few details of the weather and her day-to-day activities made keeping a diary worthwhile for her.

So, you don't need to write anything terribly personal if that's an easier way to start.

> Take care of all your memories...
> for you cannot re-live them
>
> Bob Dylan

Here are a few questions to think about before you begin:

- ? What appeals to you most, right now: writing a diary, completing lists, and answering questions, or more free-form writing?

- ? Would you prefer to write with a pen or pencil in a notebook, or type on an electronic device, or perhaps a mix of both?

- ? Is your writing for your eyes only? Would you mind others seeing it? Perhaps you'd like someone to read what you have written one day?

- ? When might be a good time for you to write: morning, afternoon, or evening? Or perhaps throughout the day when you have a spare moment, or the mood takes you?

- ? Is there a comfortable place for you to write? In your bedroom, office, kitchen, or garden?

  Or maybe you need to grab moments when you can, in the margins of your life: in a queue, on the bus, waiting for the kettle to boil, the microwave to ping, or the bath to fill?

All set? Off we go...

It's your turn to write:

Diarising development

- What did you do earlier today or yesterday?
- What was the weather like?
- Where did you go?
- What did you eat and drink? How did it taste?
- What did you observe?
- What could you hear?
- What did you think about?
- Who did you engage with?
- What would you like to remember about those people?
- How did you feel?
- What influenced your mood?
- What brightened your day?
- What made yesterday different from the day before?
- What's going on in the world that is affecting you or is of interest?
- What are your hopes for tomorrow?

Listing ideas:

- 3 most treasured possessions (that doesn't include people or pets)
- 4 favourite TV personalities
- 5 best meals you've ever eaten
- 6 films you'd happily watch again
- 7 dates in the year which are important to you
- 8 classmates from your early school days
- 9 places you'd like to spend a long weekend
- 10 people who have had a positive impact on your life

Short paragraph questions:

- Rank the seasons from your least to your most favourite. What's the reason for your preferences?
- Describe the highest place you've ever been
- If you could transform into a bird, would you be a blackbird, a flamingo, or an eagle? Why?
- What superpower would you select and what would you do with it?
- Define the word 'nice'
- A special two-legged, four-legged, or more-legged friend (of the non-human kind)
- Sunrise or sunset? Explain your choice
- Your face in the mirror

Longer writing titles:

- The oldest person in your life
- A mistake you made, but don't regret
- Something you used to be afraid of, but no longer are
- A relationship that has changed for the better over time
- A person you would have liked to get to know, but didn't
- A proud moment
- A chance encounter you would like to have
- A question you would like to be asked – and your answer

Finished? Then, set yourself some more questions to answer.

After that, share your questions with some friends and try answering each other's. You could share some answers too if you feel comfortable.

4. Essence of you

When I hatched the idea of Happy Silver People, I didn't have a lot of time on my hands. Life was divided between working and caring for Laura, interspersed with some attempts at sleeping, I had to grab moments when I could, and make them as productive as possible.

That's how the first version of the Happy Silver People logo came about, in snatched slivers of time on my phone. Here's how it evolved...

- ✔ Naturally, the starting point in terms of colour had to be silver, to represent the age group I was focusing on
- ✔ Then came yellow. This, it seemed, was a colour associated with happiness across most cultures, presumably because of the positive affiliations with sunrise and sunshine
- ✔ Could silver/grey and yellow work well together? The shades of my favourite winter scarf showed me they could, and gave me my colour palette
- ✔ For the font, I wanted something clear and easily readable. I chose Krona One, which apparently has these attributes, and it is also said to be full of personality. It was created by Yvonne Shuttler who was inspired by hand lettering on Swedish posters from the early 20th century
- ✔ Then I looked for a shape to represent a smile but struggled to find one. I did however chance upon a rainbow shape which, when turned upside down and re-coloured yellow, resembled a lopsided smile, just like my own.
- ✔ Finally, I made the text curved, following the lines of the smile.

I'm not sure that's how a professional would have done it, but I think it got me off to a distinctive start.

Here's a more recent, refreshed version which has been kindly tidied up by Michaela. She also suggested a couple of stars for balance - a bit like the sparkles in the toothpaste ads!

Now, what about transforming the Happy Silver People concept into a symbolic coat of arms? I hope you like my artistic draft on the next page.

As you can see, I've kept the silver/grey and yellow colour palette. In heraldry, silver signifies truth and sincerity (big tick), while yellow means loyalty and honour - I'll skip over, as quickly as I can with my creaky knee, a later trend for yellow to suggest cowardice,

The motto across the top says You Can Be Happy and Silver in Latin, with a sparrow beneath it, while the shield is divided into two, with the smile in one section, and a cluster of silver people in the other. For the 'supporters' of the coat of arms, I have two happy bunches of bananas.

Next up, I'm going to create a Happy Silver People bottle of cologne or perfume. It's going to be a unisex fragrance that has cheerful citrussy and bright banana-ish notes. (Actually, I hope that might smell a lot better than it sounds).

It'll be presented in a striking yellow glass container with ridged smile contours, mounted on a shiny silver base. Spray it on and spread the smiles!

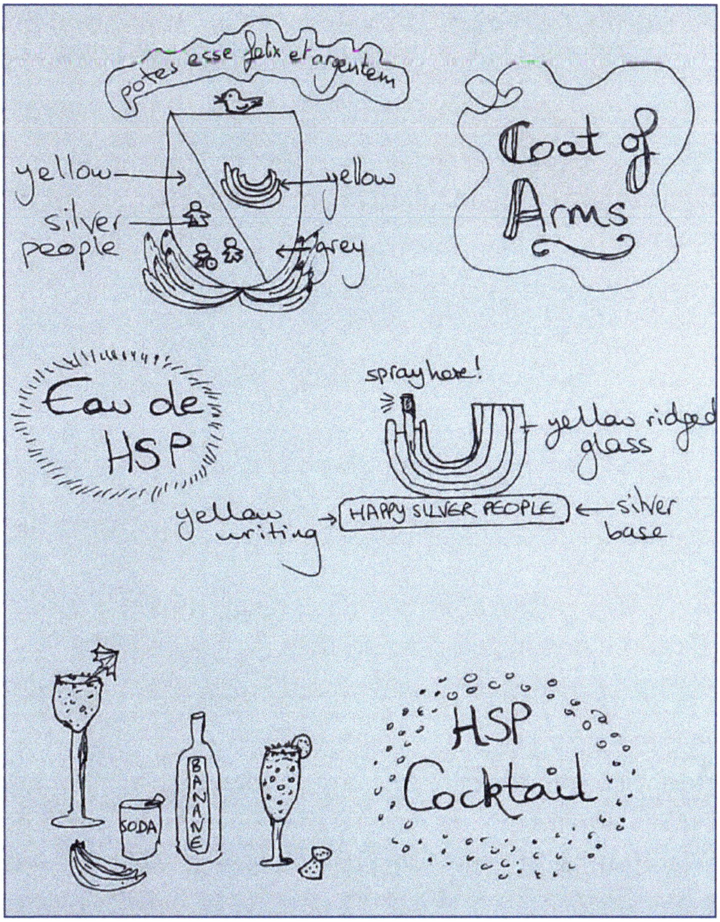

Finally, I'm turning my attention to rustling up a sunshine-y Happy Silver People cocktail and, naturally, I'm turning to my cheerful friend, the banana, for inspiration.

So, for this I am mixing, in my handy cocktail shaker, some Discarded Rum, made from banana skins. I'm blending the aromas of banana, vanilla, almond, spice, and aniseed, with the joyful bubbles of a prosecco, plus a little soda.

For a mocktail version, I'm thinking along the lines of a not-too-thick but frothy banana smoothie enhanced with vanilla essence.

I'm pouring my cocktail or mocktail mixtures into narrow flutes which have their rims decorated with delicate pieces of edible silver leaf.

I've chosen a smaller size of glass to reduce the frequency of needing to seek out the loo, and I'm not adding any ice as my teeth are sensitive.

Trust me, this is liquid happiness.

You now have four creative challenges ahead of you!

Think about the essence of 'you'.

Which attributes make you the person that you are now?

How would you encapsulate the distinctive 'you' in a logo, coat of arms, perfume or cologne, and drink or signature dish?

Your unique logo

- How will you make your logo individual and immediately recognisable?
- Which shape are you going to choose? How is it significant for you?
- What wording do you need (if any?)
- What will be your colour palette?
- For inspiration, take a look at some of the logos all around you. Why have those colours and designs been chosen for those services or products? What do they represent?

Your tailor-made coat of arms

- What will your coat of arms look like? It might be related to your logo, or something completely different.
- What will you choose as your motto? Perhaps a helpful mantra you use, or a short line from a song or poem? Which language are you going to use for it?

- How many sections will you have on your shield? Is there any significance in the number? What will go into each section?
- What's your colour scheme going to be? What's the reason?
- Who or what will be supporting your crest? Maybe a lion, a stag or a unicorn, or something more personal to you?
- What does your coat of arms say about you?

Eau de You!

- What smell are you capturing in your perfume or cologne? What are the high notes and the undertones? How will it make people feel?
- What shape and colour is the container? Is it transparent or opaque?
- Is the bottle smooth or angular? How does it feel?
- What is your essence called? Where does the name appear? How is it written?
- What's the rationale behind all your choices?

Your signature drink or dish

- What kind of taste do you want to create? Why?
- Which ingredients are you going to choose? What is the significance of your choice?
- Are there any decorative additions to your drink or dish?
- Should it be served or consumed in a particular way?
- What's your signature drink or dish called?
- Write down your recipe, along with instructions for serving and eating or drinking it.

Now consider

- ? How might your current attributes be different when you're five or ten years older?
- ? How would this impact on the evolution of your logo, coat of arms, perfume/cologne, and drink/signature dish?
- ? What can you do to ensure you have the attributes you'd like to have in the future?

5. Least said ...

Have you ever wondered what the first words our ancestors used to communicate may have been? Surely, 'Help!' and 'WOLF!' would have been top of the list?

Well, it seems not. Perhaps a general emergency howl would have got the point across in times of danger.

Researchers from Reading University* have identified words that were common across at least four of the seven language families of Europe and Asia 15,000 years ago, and neither of these two warnings makes the cut.

So, can you guess some of the twenty-three earliest words** which got conversations flowing back then?

Let's create your language pack:

- Choose two of these: mother, father, baby, man
- And one of these: hand, head, nose, foot
- Three of these: wood, bark, fire, smoke, ashes,
- Four of these: that, this, who, what, when, why, where
- Five of these: eat, give, flow, hear, pull, push, see, spit
- Two of these: black, green, white, red, old, young, happy, sad
- And, finally, one from this selection: tiger, horse, cat, bird, worm, spider

Put your choices in the box below. I'm feeling benevolent today and have given you another five to start you off:

not	you	I	we	go

What do you think the next twelve words might have been? Perhaps "Please", "Thanks", and ten words about the weather?

You get to choose, to bring your vocabulary up to forty words:

1	7
2	8
3	9
4	10
5	11
6	12

* Atkinson, Q.A., Calude, A.S., Meade, A., Pagel, M. (2021) '*Ultraconserved words point to deep language ancestry across Eurasia'* in *PNAS* Vol 110, No 21

It's 15,000 years ago

The big thaw is underway at the end of the Ice Age.

Your sabretooth headphones have picked up the fireside chat of a group of hunter-gatherers, having dinner outside their caves.

Script their meaningful dialogue, using as many of your forty words as you can. You can include an unlimited number of noises, gestures, and actions.

And now we're back in the present day

- ? Which are your own 'common core' words?
- ? Are there any words or expressions you find yourself over-using?
- ? Are there alternatives you could use, or could you remove them completely?
- ? Are there times when it would be useful to put your message across more concisely?
- ? How could you start developing the good habits you need in order to be clearer and more concise?

**The actual 23 words which have been identified as being common across at least four of the seven language families of Europe and Asia 15,000 years ago are: mother, man, hand, fire, ashes, bark, that, this, who, what, give, hear, pull, flow, spit, black, old, worm, I, thou, ye, we, not

6. Wordilicious

We've been thinking about how our ancestors might have used a minimal number of words to communicate. We're now going to exercise our silvery-grey cells in a different way, by exploring how we can continue to use and extend our vocabulary as we grow older.

There are around half a million words in the English language, with new ones being added all the time.

Here's an evocative example from the decade I was born: the word petrichor was coined by two Australians to describe the pleasant earthy smell which arises when rain falls on dry soil. It combines the Ancient Greek words petra, meaning rock, with ichor, the mythical golden fluid in the blood of the gods. If I close my eyes and take a deep breath, I know just what they were trying to capture.

Let me share some other concepts which we don't have a word for in English (yet). As I do, you can think about the situations when these additions to your vocabulary would have come in handy...

- Ever felt an overwhelming urge to hug or squeeze something cute - maybe a playful puppy or a baby's chubby little cheeks? That sensation is called gigil in Tagalog

- You had an indentation left on your skin from wearing something tight – just like my favourite jeans with the waistband that starts digging in as soon as food passes my lips. That ridge mark is described as a keralu in Tulu (spoken in the southern part of India)

- Maybe one you'd rather forget, if you were the victim of a disastrous haircut that made you look worse than before. That's captured in the word age-otori (pronounced ah-jey-oh-toh-ree) in Japanese. Ah, the memories of my fringe being butchered a few weeks before my wedding come flooding back!

- Hopefully, you've never followed through on a schnapsidee. This German word literally means a 'schnapps idea', the sort of ridiculous plan someone might come up with when they're drunk. I'm sure an example or two from my own experience isn't needed to illustrate the point.

- When did you last experience zhaghzhagh? A wonderful Persian word, this describes the uncontrollable chattering of teeth, either because of the cold - or a tidal wave of rage!

- Here's a helpful one. It's the Scottish verb to tartle. This captures your hesitation while you trying to remember someone's name. It doesn't apply if you forget the name completely, but just that brief awkward moment of brain-rummaging as you try to retrieve it.

- Do you recognise either of these characteristics in the people around you – or perhaps these words could be used to describe you?

  In Italian, an attaccabottoni (literally 'attach buttons') is that garrulous person who traps you in a corner to generously share every detail of their life, while in Swedish a tidsoptimist (literally a 'time optimist') is someone who is always late because they think they have far more time than they really do.

- Here are three powerful words related to nature that conjure up not just images, but sounds, smells, and feelings too.

  There's listopad, which in Russian describes the falling of leaves; gökotta which in Swedish means waking up at dawn and going outside, just to hear birds chirping; and vedriti, a Slovenian word to convey when you shelter from the rain. It can also be used metaphorically, such as when you're in a bad mood and 'sheltering', as you wait for the negative emotions to pass.

- An important one for me, with my love of smiley bananas, is pisan zapra. In Malay, this means the time it takes to eat a banana, which apparently, is roughly two minutes.

- Naturally, we need a Finnish word to finish. The spectacularly spelt hyppytyynytyydytys means 'bouncy cushion satisfaction' and describes the joy of sitting or bouncing up and down on a springy cushion. The good news is that you don't have to be fluent in Finnish to adopt this wonderful word!

Which words do you feel are missing from your vocabulary, and maybe from the English language?

My father's favourite insult for other car drivers who didn't behave in the way he expected, was a loud and heartfelt, "Bladder-headed ass!"

No, it's not in the dictionary. Yet.

? Now note down the memories, feelings, or images that the words above conjure up for you

? Which ones will you be adding to your vocabulary?

? Which other words do you use, or have you heard, that you would like to add to the English dictionary?

? How can you continue to enrich the range of words you use as you grow older?

7. Heavenly 17

It's time to pick a number, any number! Well, perhaps best between 5 and 20. Then we'll take a look at how that number relates to your life - in numerous different ways.

I'm taking number 17 as an example. What's my reason for choosing this particular number? It's because I joined an online group called TEAM17* and, as a way to introduce myself to everyone, I wrote a 17-related post each weekend for 17 weeks.

Here are some of the ways in which the number 17 has had resonance for me:

Page 17

At the time, I was drafting Happy Silver People and had just completed page 17, all about sounds in the silence. The 17th line of that draft read 'clocks ticking'. Phew, no pressure!

17 attempts

I recalled my determination to get up on water skis, many years before, in the murk of the Johore Straits, off Singapore. It took me 17 long lessons to control those skis and, strangely, the instructor never once mentioned that we were in crocodile-infested waters.

Advice I'd give to 17-year-old me

- Think about what the careers advisor will tell you in a year or two. There's a great option on that list – don't dismiss it because you're not sure what it is!
- Please start a pension plan in your 20s
- And start wearing sunscreen and sunglasses
- Buy a EuroMillions lottery ticket for 8 Oct 2019. Try numbers 7, 10, 15, 44, and 19, with 3 and 12 as your lucky stars
- Ditch the self-doubt, take a deep breath, and put yourself out there!

What advice would my 17-year-old self give back to 60-year-old me, I wonder?

Challenge 17

Could I lose 17lbs in 17 weeks? Good question! You'll find out in a later section...

17 years ago

By December, going back 17 years took me to Laura's first Christmas Eve. In Bethlehem's atmospheric Church of the Nativity, the air was heavy with incense and chanting, and, with midnight approaching, ever more worshippers poured in.

We decided to leave, but the aisles and main entrances were all impassable. Finally, we pushed our way to a tiny wooden door in a side chapel and, bent double, squeezed our way outside.

Straightening up in the cold night air, we realised we were nose-to-nose with a huge, compressed crowd hoping to be allowed in through this low entrance.

With no hope of moving forward, I pulled myself up onto a narrow ledge running around the side of the church at waist height.

As the Big Yorkshire Silverback passed Laura up to me in her carry seat, the crowd fell suddenly fell silent. I looked around, anxiously. What was wrong?

A low murmur started at the front and grew, and grew. I strained my ears and caught the Arabic words, 'It's a baby! It's a baby!' being said over and over again.

Hands were raised and Laura's seat was lifted up high and passed back gently over the heads of strangers. Other arms reached out to support me, and then the BYS, as we negotiated our way along the ledge.

When I reached the fringe of the crowd and jumped down, I was presented with Laura, the only baby we saw in Bethlehem that night.

Items spelling out SEVENTEEN

Which random items could I find around the house to spell out the word 'seventeen'?

Silver sixpences

Energy pulse point oil. Not so sure it still works?

Vesuvius lava, polished and set into a brooch which was Grannie Gwen's

Earwax remover. Yes, this works!

Noah's Ark, carved from Palestinian olive wood. Not full-size.

Tulip tree wood from Pennsylvania. William Penn is connected to my home village and sent trees back to the community. They grow to their full height after 200 years and symbolise liberty and democracy.

Elf ears, two. Discovered, with twenty-one others (right ones only), when tidying Dad's office. Where did all the left ones go?

Electricity-generating machine from Victorian times. Powered by magnets, it was designed to give anyone with a 'nervous condition' a small shock when they held the two handles. I can confirm it worked when we were kids.

Notebook. Ready to capture any brilliant ideas which come to me in the middle of the night. In pristine condition.

Now, what was the happy silver benefit of all this number-inspired activity? I could quickly rustle up a list of 17 positives but, essentially, this was a fresh filter through which I could view my world: an interesting exercise for my little silver brain cells, a different prompt for my memory, and a new reason to explore my cupboards, bookshelves, and photo albums. It was quite fun too!

*TEAM 17 is led by one of the top professional speakers and success coaches in the world: the mighty, the marvellous, the mega-motivational Michael Heppell. To discover read one of his books, such as Flip It, and find him online with the How to Be Brilliant group.

What is the resonance for you in these 17-related references?

When you were 17

17 weeks

1917 or 2017

The 17th letter forwards: Q and the 17th letter backwards: O

Atomic number 17: chlorine

A date including 17

17 years in the future

17 bingo call: Dancing Queen by Abba

An address with 17 in it

17 steps – where does this take you?

17 days, hours, or minutes

17 years ago

A phrase or name with 17 letters

Items spelling out SEVENTEEN

A 17th anniversary

Page 17, line 17

£17m, £17k, £17 or 17p

The 17th country alphabetically:

counting forwards (Belgium) and backwards (Tunisia)

A 17-related challenge

- Don't forget to share your answers with a friend – or 17.
- Then pick another number between 5 and 20, and start all over again!

8. Making an exhibition for yourself

As I was going to St Ives, I met... Angela!

An artist and old family friend, Angela was also walking along the beach at low tide, against a backdrop of quaint cottages, fishing boats, and excitable, sandy dogs. She was heading off later to see an exhibition of vibrant, abstract work by one of her inspirations, Patrick Heron.

Knowing next to nothing about modern art, I was pleased to accept an invitation to join her in the hope she could enlighten me. And she did. She enthusiastically explained the significance of the artist's choices - the colours, the shades, the contrasts, the shapes, the lines, the angles - and how those decisions then worked together. I gained some insights and was able to appreciate abstract art in a way I hadn't been able to before.

In return, I shared my love of sculpture, especially large-scale pieces: art you can get up close to and experience through touch. It can be even better if the artwork is outdoors: framed by its environment, it is ever-changing. Daybreak and dusk, mist and rain, crows cawing or the breath of a breeze, the warmth of the sun and the chill of autumn, all contribute to a multi-sensory experience.

I have a particular penchant for shiny sculptures (I like the idea of being a sparrow, but suspect there's a little bit of magpie in me too). That mirrored surface means the viewer is reflected in the artwork, and so becomes part of it, just for a while. It makes each viewing not only unique, but personalised.

My favourite exhibitions have included the oversize work of Spanish artist, Jaume Plensa. His huge figures composed of a latticework of letters of the alphabet, sat on the hillside at Yorkshire Sculpture Park while nature provided a constantly changing backdrop. And the Sotheby's displays in the gardens of Chatsworth House, with exhibits such as a curvy, steel statue called Marilyn

Monroe and a huge. smooth heart shape, Love Me, both by Richard Hudson.

Where would I love to visit next? Top of the list is Naoshima, the tiny Japanese art island in the Seto Inland Sea, followed by the intriguingly named Museum of Broken Relationships in Croatia – I'll be sure to pack my waterproof mascara, and perhaps a trot around the Museum of Bad Art in Massachusetts would cheer me up afterwards.

Otherwise, I'll need some scuba-diving lessons before I head off to the Cancun Underwater Museum in Mexico, featuring 500 submerged sculptural pieces made of marine-friendly materials beneath the waves.

Other options? There's the International Spy Museum in Washington DC, the Bata Shoe Museum in Canada, the Gold Museum in Bogota, the NASA Museum in Langley, the Ramen Museum in Yokohama celebrating the instant noodle, and the Sulabh International Museum of Toilets in New Delhi which demonstrates the evolution over 5000 years of this essential but often (wrongly) under-appreciated feature in our lives.

Oh, how I would love to curate an exhibition of my own. Wouldn't you?

Well, congratulations! Look down at what you're holding between your thumb and first finger. It's a stiff, white, gold-edged card. Now read that swirly black writing. It's inviting you and your guests to a VIP opening of the exhibition of the century! Oh, and the reason for the invitation is that you have been the driving force behind the whole event!

Do tell us more!

- ? **What is the theme of your exhibition?** Does it bring together the work of one person, one community, or one culture? Is there a style, period of time or development through the ages which links the exhibits? Do they all relate to a shared concept in some way, such as a homage to bananas?

? **What does your exhibition feature?** Drawings, landscapes, portraits, seascapes, oils, watercolours, drawings, data, photographs, calligraphy, china, sports equipment, stamps, flowers, interactive displays, performances?

? **Where is your exhibition located?** Perhaps in the centre of a capital city, or on a mountain peak, or deep underground?

? **What is your display space like?** How does it look, smell, sound, and feel? How do your visitors experience the exhibits?

? **What's the purpose of your exhibition?** What would you like your visitors to feel when they leave, and to do as a result?

? **What is the name of your exhibition?** How and where does that name appear?

Draw an aerial plan to show how your exhibition is set out

Sketch some snapshots of:

- the first impressions your visitors will get
- what they will see part-way through
- the final image that your visitors will take away with them

How could you create an echo of your exhibition in your own home or garden?

☺

Exploring an exhibition every couple of months could be a great way to keep your mind active and open to new experiences and perspectives. Plus, you'll not be stuck for something to talk about. How could you develop this habit?

9. Poetry in motion

How do you feel about writing poetry? Perhaps the idea seems daunting, or just 'not for you'. Maybe you see poetry as too deep and meaningful, saccharinely sentimental, or pretentiously obscure with an over-elaborate manipulation of words, resulting in an impenetrable briar of text. A bit like the interminably long drum and guitar solos on album tracks performed by self-indulgent shaggy-haired musicians in the '70s.

After a fifty-year break, I've been having fun writing some poetry. To show you how talented a wordsmith I was while growing up, here is the pinnacle of my endeavours, dating from when I was eight. I felt immensely proud that this was deemed good enough to be published in the annual school magazine:

It came in handy a few years later when I'd left it a bit late to write my English homework on a Sunday evening and lacked inspiration. Yes, I plagiarized my own childhood homework. As the work of a fourteen-year-old, it didn't seem to dazzle my teacher quite so much: I earned a perfunctory tick, but no enthusiastic and encouraging comment.

Five decades later, I decided to try a haiku poem or two. This Japanese form of poetry has a set structure with just three lines. The rhythm is of five syllables (beats) for the first and third lines, and seven for the middle one – which makes 17 in all!

Traditionally, haiku has a seasonal reference and a 'cutting word' in each line and there are some truly beautiful examples, old and new. Fortunately for a novice like me, though, addressing broader subject matter is now more acceptable.

My first haiku attempts to capture the process of writing, while the second describes catching moments in time to be creative!

Thoughts form, then flow, from
head and heart, to pen and page,
channelled into print

I love the haiku!
So short that you could write one
Sitting on the loo

I also wanted to explore the idea of telling a short story through a more free-form poem, and came up with this true tale of Grandfer Cyril just for you:

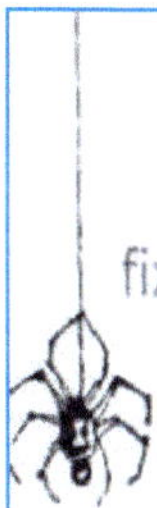

Grandfather, on waking,
fumbles for his dentures,
fixedly smiling on his bedside cabinet
in the pre-dawn gloom.
A bony finger
swiftly slides the top teeth in,
his thumb following through
with a firm upward push.
Bitterness floods the roof of his mouth:
The taste of a spider,
surprised in its sleep.

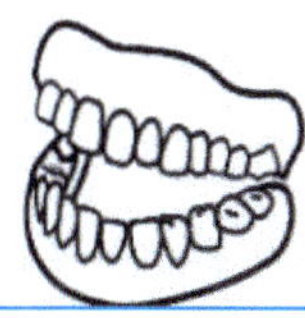

Please don't let a dislike or distrust of poetry from decades ago define your prowess today! It's never too late to try your hand at a haiku, share a story in a new shape, or read aloud a rhyming rap.

Poetry should be for everyone. Remember:

On this straight street some poets live,
Down that leafy lane there live some too.
They call themselves by many names.
They look like me; they look like you

How do you fancy writing a poem that rhymes? Let's being with words ending in '-ation'.

Here's a starter pack for you, but there are plenty more words you can add. Even constipation if that's your inclination!

creation	valuation	determination	nation	domination
demonstration	occupation	admiration	ovation	
cancelation	medication	dedication	liquidation	
situation	celebration	murmuration	emancipation	
evacuation	beautification	manifestation	location	
fluctuation	station	imagination	frustration	
provocation	restoration	revelation	evaluation	
multiplication	graduation	duplication	saturation	

Now get ready with your idea generation
Add joining words, to give some inter-relation
Don't worry too much about your punctuation -
You'll soon be a poetry sensation!

10. Named and framed

I hope by now you feel that there is a least a little spark of creativity within you to start exploring, or that your existing creativity might be extended into new directions.

To finish this theme, let's have some fun with these five letters. Add whatever you like to turn them into doodles of:

- an animal, bird, or fish
- a person
- a plant
- something you eat and
- something decorative.

You choose which letter to transform for each.

a e i o u

Here's my effort: a becomes a vine; e is a weird fish, i is a tree, o is an egg, and u becomes a waist and an arm.

After warming up with our vowels, let's move on to creating several masterpieces to hang in the Happy Silver Gallery.

Here are your themes, with a few ideas as to how you might interpret them...

A. A landscape

Maybe a favourite countryside or city scene, or a special place you visited long ago?

B. A water scene

Perhaps a tempestuous sea, a peaceful pond, or the wonders of life beneath the waves?

C. Nature

Leafy woodland, dense jungle, wild animals in the savannah, rain on the window, or your unique take on a traditional bowl of fruit?

D. People

A family meal, friends out together, strangers at an airport, or the queue for the number 17 bus?

E. A time of year

An important date in the calendar, a festival, or features of a particular season?

F. A portrait

A special person, a beloved pet, or perhaps yourself?

G. A theme of your choice

We've provided a selection of frames in which you can display your artwork - you choose which frame to use for the different themes.

Don't forget to give each of your masterpieces a title!

TITLE:

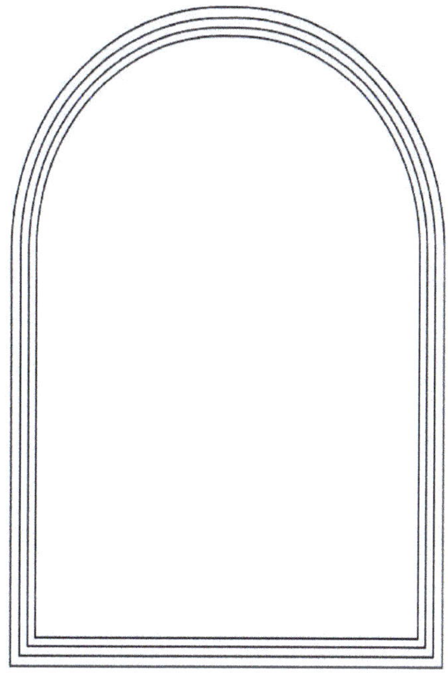

TITLE:

TITLE:

TITLE:

TITLE:

TITLE:

TITLE:

Looking after yourself

1. Silver cells
2. Don’t get the hump
3. The joy of sox
4. The biting point
5. Gut, glorious gut
6. Taking the strain
7. Hi ho silver dining
8. Shake up your drinks
9. Weight on me
10. The egg tooth

Go to the Happy Silver People website if you’d like to download task sheets for this section

1. Silver cells

Let me stop you right there. Yes, you. Now, please.

Before you venture any further, go and take a look at a photo of yourself from around ten years ago.

Don't worry, I'll wait here until you get back.

What can you see?

The picture I'm looking at shows a dark-haired me, slimmed down enough to get back into my wedding dress for our fifteenieth anniversary - although I did need the assistance of suck-it-in undergarments and some not-so-gentle manhandling from friends.

All the people in my photos from that event are completely different now. Aside from being older, hopefully wiser, and possibly wider, they are different people in that just about every cell in their body has been replaced in the past decade. This is literally one of those occasions when you can use the word 'literally' about the difference, and be literally right.

Our bodies, of course, change and regenerate throughout our lives. Although the process may not be as dramatic as a gecko re-generating a shed tail, a spider replacing a mislaid leg, or a Highland stag growing a whole new rack of antlers, it's pretty amazing all the same.

We probably notice it most when we observe babies getting bigger and bonnier, our nails growing longer, or healthy new skin appearing after a scab drops off or a blister bursts.

But there's a plenitude of other ways that our bodies change over time, with cells being replaced at different rates, depending on the work we expect them to do for us.

Let's consider these extraordinary examples:

- 0.1mm a day: the growth of your fingernails
- 0.35mm a day: the growth of your head hair
- 1mm a month: the growth of your toenails
- 1 day: your cornea can regenerate itself, although other parts of your eye won't change
- 5 days: the cells which line your stomach walls and intestines are replaced. These cells have a short, difficult life as they are exposed to corrosive acids in your stomach
- 2 to 4 weeks: your outer layer of skin is regenerated after experiencing all sorts of wear and tear
- 4 months: your red blood cells are replaced after a tough journey through your circulatory system, as they carry oxygen to tissues all around your body
- 150 to 500 days: your liver cells are replaced to ensure they can remain immune to toxins and can continue detoxifying your body effectively
- 3 to 6 years: the lifespan of the hair on your body is around three years for men and six years for women
- Every 6 years: certain cells in your heart are replaced
- Every 10 years: your skeleton is replaced. These cells regenerate almost constantly but the complete process takes about a decade. This slows as we age, so our bones get thinner and weaker.
- at 30 years old: your pancreatic beta cells stopped growing
- at 10 years old: the growth of your heart muscle cells stopped
- at 3 years old: your cerebellum grey matter ceased growing
- at birth: the growth of your visual cortex halted. This means that the cells in the lenses you are using to look at this page right now, are the same as the ones you were born with!

How amazing that our bodies are refreshed constantly – and perhaps even more astonishing is that the same sense of 'me' and 'you', with our personal memories, likes and dislikes, hopes and fears, foibles, and idiosyncrasies, remains!

With all that cell regeneration constantly going on, why on earth do we not stay eternally young? Unfortunately, the influx of fresh cells is not like a drip feed of long-life serum.

Gradually the tips of our DNA, which carry the instructions for cell processes, start to fray and mutations develop which are then passed on to new cells.

The regeneration of cells becomes progressively unreliable until, eventually, there is no more cell division. This is what we call the process of ageing.

How about our brain cells? The same neurons in our cerebral cortex, the brain's outer layer which governs memory, thought, language, attention, and consciousness, stay with us from our birth to our death. As they are not replaced, loss or deterioration of these cells over our lifetime can lead to conditions such as dementia.

Importantly, however, other parts of the brain, such as the hippocampus which helps us learn, and the olfactory bulb which helps us smell, can rejuvenate. Hooray!

If I think of grey matter, I immediately picture a gloopy, drab mess. And that soupy sludge is in a saucepan, being stirred by my student flatmate, Lisa, who is creating a papier mâché rhinoceros head for a fancy dress party at Edinburgh Zoo.

Fortunately, it seems that our 'little grey cells' as Hercule Poirot was so fond of calling them, are not as I imagine them.

Grey matter makes up 40% of our brains, with white matter making up the other 60%. The grey matter contains most of the brain's neuronal cells, while the white helps to connect the grey areas, so that information can be conducted, processed, and then sent to other parts of the body. In essence, the grey matter is where the processing is done, and the white matter provides the channels of communication.

How can we keep our brain cells active and encourage them to continue making new connections?

- by stimulating our senses so that they preserve the links they have to existing memories, and creating fresh paths to new ones
- by inspiring ourselves to be creative, develop new skills, and think differently
- by looking after our mental and physical health
- by valuing and engaging with the world around us
- by embracing opportunities to explore new experiences
- by re-connecting with others and considering fresh perspectives.

Well. how amazing! These are all themes we're looking at in this book!

Here are ten top tips for keeping your brain cells firing and re-wiring:

- Read books, but maybe not your usual ones. Choose novels by where they are set, explore a different fiction genre, or pick non-fiction on a subject you know little about

- Play card games, board games, even video games which hold your attention and get you thinking ahead

- Do crosswords, jigsaws, and other puzzles each day

- Set yourself alphabetical listing activities – the A to Z of animals, colours, bands, fruit and vegetables, movies, sports teams or players, actors, authors, countries, cars, song titles, rivers, flowers, drinks, cities, song titles...

- Try out tasks using your non-dominant hand, from doing up buttons to writing your alphabetical lists

- Learn a new language - or how to say happy birthday in fifty different languages, if you prefer

- Get physically active. It seems aerobic exercise may increase brain volume in ageing humans. If you can combine it with learning a routine, be it tai chi or line dancing, so much the better

- Fast occasionally. It doesn't have to be for a whole day – you can give your digestive system a longer than usual break between your last meal on one day and your first meal the next. There are signs that fasting could support existing neurons in your brain to survive, while encouraging the growth of new ones, plus the development of the synapses which carry messages between them. This might contribute to preventing cognitive impairment and conditions linked to Alzheimer's

- Sleep well. Lack of sleep is known to have a negative impact on our cognitive ability, making it harder to think and remember. To keep our grey matter functioning effectively, we should aim to get around eight hours of good-quality sleep each night

- Meditate twice a week for around twenty minutes. Those who meditate long-term may increase the grey matter in their brains, possibly because they are more relaxed and so have more restful sleep.

However, you choose to exercise your little silver cells, make sure it's something you enjoy!

> Some days
> I amaze myself
>
> Other days
> I look for my phone
> while I'm talking into it
>
> I've forgotten who said this

2. Don't get the hump

Unless you're Columbo, I'm guessing you're probably not going to welcome having a hunch.

Growing older brings with it a danger of developing what is known as a dowager's or buffalo hump. I can see the doughty dowager resplendent in a twin set, tweed skirt, and stout shoes facing off a burly, bearded buffalo, snorting and pawing the ground (the buffalo, not the dowager), as they prepare to fight over whose name should be attached to the lamentable lump at the base of our necks.

Poor posture with a forward bend can weaken our upper back muscles and create that hump. I can sense the early stage of a hump-ette now, as I uncoil after slumping and slouching during another Zoom call. When I un-hunch and sit back in my chair, like a baddie cradling a cat in a James Bond film, I hear a cacophony of cracking and creaking emanating from my neck and shoulders.

What are the benefits of good posture?

- ✔ It makes us look and feel alert and engaged, taller and slimmer, more confident, and capable. Perhaps the kind of impression we are even keener to make as we grow older?
- ✔ Our bones and joints are kept aligned, meaning we use our muscles correctly and avoid joints wearing abnormally, possibly leading to arthritis
- ✔ It prevents stress on ligaments, backache, and muscular pain
- ✔ Our lungs have more capacity, so we can breathe more efficiently
- ✔ Our organs have the space they need to digest our food properly
- ✔ We have better circulation and core strength
- ✔ We are less fatigued, tense, and stressed; more productive, focused, and relaxed
- ✔ It may improve our memory too!

So, as much as I adore elderly aristocratic ladies and animals that roam the plains, I really don't want a dowager or a buffalo to sweep into my life in quite this way.

Plus, as a wise person once said: give me a home where the buffalo roam, and I'll show you a very messy carpet.

What can you do to prevent getting the hump – or even reverse it?

- Stand more often, such as whenever you make a call. Keep your back straight and hold your stomach in!

- When sitting, keep your back and thighs at right angles. You can practise this by sitting on a peanut ball while you're watching TV

- Whether sitting or standing, move as much as you can and give your muscles a good stretch every twenty minutes

- Try this exercise: stand with your back against a wall, your heels, lower back, back of your head, and shoulders all touching it. Drop your shoulders once, twice, three times until relaxed. Then place your elbows against the wall with the backs of your hands touching it too. Your challenge is to raise your arms, with your elbows and backs of your hands maintaining in contact with the wall. Raise them out to the sides, then above your head so that your hands join; then bring them back down, touching the wall all the way. Some days I still struggle to do this, but I definitely feel the difference when I get it right!

- Consider working at a standing desk – there are now good value adjustable ones available, so you can switch from a conventional sitting arrangement to standing, and then back again, quite easily. Get professional advice as to whether this might be right for you – standing all day may put stress and strain on other parts of your body, so identifying the right set-up for you is important

- Try using a kneeling or rocking chair when working (no, not the type Val Doonican used to sit in while crooning in a patterned sweater). These chairs are designed to help you sit in a more upright, but comfortable, position and could be alternated with a more traditional supportive chair

- Ensure your diet includes calcium-rich foods which will help reduce the risk of osteoporosis, as this can exacerbate the impact of poor posture. Look for dairy produce such as yoghurt, milk, and hard cheese, but also sardines and tinned salmon, plus almonds, dried figs, and green veggies such as kale, broccoli, cabbage, and okra (one of my fave Indian side dishes)

- Join an online or face-to-face yoga class to get specific guidance. You may find end up setting yourself new challenges, such as doing the splits in six months!

- If you have limited mobility or are a wheelchair user there are exercises you can do to achieve many of the benefits outlined above. Speak to your doctor or physio to find out what would be suitable for you to do

- If you're concerned that, rather than developing a fatty hump because of poor posture, you may be suffering from scoliosis, osteoporosis, or another condition affecting your neck and spine, make sure you check it out with your doctor.

> If your spine is inflexibly stiff at 30, you are old.
> If it is completely flexible at 80, you are young.
>
> Joseph Pilates

3. The joy of sox

Over six decades my feet have served me well. They have been up mountains, through jungles, and across burning coals for charity; squashed into winklepickers, unsupported in pumps, and elevated in platform boots; gorged on by leeches in Borneo, savaged by sea urchins in New Zealand, and nibbled by fish in a nail salon in Sheffield.

I am pleased that, despite my increasing girth, I'm able to see my precious feet, and my toes are just within reach of my outstretched fingers. I feel we still have a connection. But maybe it's time I had a chat to my two long-suffering friends to see how they are doing.

Hello, feet! How are you feeling now you're in the sixtieth year of taking me around? I hope you're up for a quick Q&A session to help me prepare for the rest of our time together.

Q: My shoe size has stayed the same since I stopped growing in height. Is that likely to change?

A: You may need a bigger shoe size in time, but that'll be because we have got wider rather than longer. We're not as elastic as we once were, you know. As our tissue is less tight, we may splay out and our arches may sag too. Much like the rest of you!

Q: Hmm, I was hoping for happy feet, but looks like I've got cheeky feet instead. OK, does your weakening tissue mean I'm more likely to injure you two?

A: Yes, it's possible. As our tissue starts to collapse, you may get arthritis and pain in your feet, so we would love more support. You won't necessarily have to fling out your flip-flops or hang up your high heels, but if we're getting unstable or painful underneath, please consider more comfortable footwear.

We now dream of shoes with a little bit of arch support, and ones which don't bend too much – you shouldn't be able to fold them in half. Oh, and a thicker sole, more than just a few millimetres, would be heaven.

If wearing heels is necessary, please ensure you vary the height. We both agree our ideal heels would be around one and a half inches high. Like you, we love a variety of footwear, not the same shape and style every day.

Q: I'm coming round to your way of thinking about what makes a great shoe. I must confess I've noticed pain under the ball of my right foot a few times. There also seems to be an invisible magnet pulling my knees together when I stand still, making you splay out a bit. What's going on down there, below the ankle line?

A: Yes, that pain can be pretty intense! Remember when you couldn't walk for a week because of it, and hobbled round to A&E convinced you'd broken a bone in your foot?

You know what your problem is? It's Fat Pad Atrophy. As you've noticed, getting older has brought with it some additional body padding, but ironically there is one place where you're actually losing padding, and it's right where you'd rather keep it: here, on your feet. The fat pads on the balls of your feet are thinning, and what's left doesn't protect us as we pound the pavements each day. That brings us paaaaaaaain!

It also sounds like you're describing Adult Acquired Flat Foot, where we start turning outwards over time as the tendons become weaker. It's common in middle age. The tendons which are meant to support your arches stop working, causing us feet to become flat.

A giveaway sign is that, from behind, other people can now see most of your toes jutting out at the side, whereas before it would only be the two outer ones on each foot. Injuries, obesity, diabetes, and high blood pressure can also lead to flatter feet.

Q: So, what else should I be aware of?

A: Let me walk you through five other conditions that we would be hoping to avoid as you grow older...

First off is Plantar Fasciitis. That's stiffness and pain you'd feel underneath your heel, especially first thing in the morning. The plantar fascia is a long ligament that runs along the sole and supports your arch. It can be irritated by repeated stress, such as running (unlikely in your case, admittedly). Having high arches or being overweight could also make you more susceptible to it.

Next up is Achilles Tendinitis. The Achilles is the tendon you use to flex your foot when you climb stairs or go up on your toes, but age and lowered blood supply can weaken it, causing your heel or the back of your ankle to hurt. Watch out - it doesn't only affect athletes and runners!

Third on our list is Morton's Neuroma. It's a surprisingly common foot condition, possibly affecting as many as one in three people, particularly women who wear high heels or shoes which squeeze their toes. It leads to pain in the front part of the foot or a feeling like you're walking on a rock or a marble – sounds worse than that time you trod on Lovely Laura's Duplo bricks.

In at number four is osteoarthritis, which mostly affects people over sixty-five. It occurs when cartilage, a flexible tissue that prevents friction, breaks down so that bone now rubs against bone. You might get arthritis in the middle of your foot, which sets in when the arch starts to sag and collapse, or there's big toe arthritis when you can get a bump on top of the joint. Gout is another painful form of arthritis and is one foot condition that is more common in men. A waste product called uric acid collects as crystals, often in the big toe, so that it swells, stiffens, and hurts. More than childbirth. Apparently.

Finally, there are bone spurs and bunions which cause pain along the inside of your foot at the joint where your big toe meets your foot. With bunions, the bones are out of place so the big toe angles outwards, while with bone spurs, there are growths at the edge of the bones, which can push on nearby nerves and tissues as they grow. These conditions can worsen after the age of sixty and may be linked to the changes in muscle structure and relaxation of the tissues.

We can't tiptoe around the fact that you'll become more susceptible to some nasty foot conditions as you age. Don't let that stop you from being active, though!

Q: Those all sound very painful and unpleasant. What else could I be doing now to look after you better, my two podiatric friends?

A: Exercise your feet and toes – tensing and relaxing the muscles, spreading them out as far as you can, and getting your toes moving up and down. Some barefoot walking may help too. Try strengthening exercises too, like trying to pick up a piece of paper or small objects with your toes.

Give your calf muscles a stretch as well. A few minutes in the morning and again before bed will help to loosen them up. This can reduce the amount of force you're putting through the joints of your foot and ankle; having greater ankle movement in turn means less stress on the smaller joints of the foot.

Also, check for fungal infections, as older people can be more susceptible. Treat any itching or scaling on the soles of your feet as, if left, it may spread to your toenails. Fungus can be really hard to kill so use medication for as long as you're told.

Bear in mind that, over time, it may well become more difficult for you to get up close to your feet, so make an extra effort to keep us clean and fresh, and don't forget to dry between your toes!

Q: OK, I don't think I'll drag my feet over adopting those activities. But what would it take to make you both really, really happy feet?

A: Over the past sixty years, we may have walked 90,000 miles together. I'm not sure we would walk 90,000 more.

A bit of extra pampering wouldn't go amiss. Your more mature skin makes less oil and elastin, so it's drier and less supple than before, and your heels are more at risk of hardening and cracking. So, use some special cream to exfoliate the tough top layer, then give us a gentle scrub with a pumice stone or file to remove dead skin. Please moisturise and massage us every day.

You could help boost our circulation by using a pressure pad, or your Shakti mat. It might take a while to get used to standing on the sharp points – start with your socks on - but doing this for a few minutes a day can help release tension and boost your blood flow.

And how about investing in some more of those super-sensitive socks, with absolutely no seams or ribbing to bother us? Soft tops are also rather sublime, and you don't get an unsightly keralu or two when you slip them off (check back to the Wordilicous section, if you've forgotten).

Even better are the pairs of socks which have a designated right and left, and it's printed along the sole. And even more betterer are the ones with a little bit of embroidery to tell you which one is which when you are putting them on in the dark. Oh, joy!

Q: Thank you so much, dear feet, for giving me those pedestrian insights. Shall I pop some fluffy sleep socks on you, ready for bedtime?

A: Oh, yes, please. We're on our last legs after all that talking.

Now, dear reader, I will leave you to have your own private conversation with your feet...

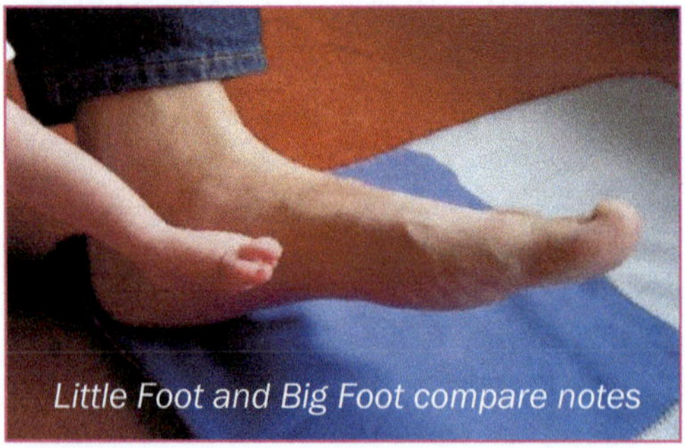

Little Foot and Big Foot compare notes

4. The biting point

Here I am, approaching sixty and yet still teething like a baby. That final wisdom tooth, impacted in my lower right mandible, keeps making its grumbly presence felt. I appreciate a little more why babies can be so grouchy and grizzly. It's not much fun when your gums are split, swollen, and sore, your nose is running a marathon, and a concrete post seems to be trying to push its way through your jawbone at glacial speed.

And yet, it could be worse. Consider the garden snail with around 14,000 teeth arranged in rows on its tongue and a complete inability to use a toothbrush. Or the snarly shark who loses at least one tooth a week, and presumably is therefore perpetually teething. Or the giraffe with thirty-two teeth, just like us, but none of them top and front. Not the most flattering look for a human, but seemingly quite a fetching feature for these lofty ruminants; one which would have potential partners swiping left on the dating app Giraffder.

Our teeth are amazingly strong. Admittedly, not as strong as the teeth of the limpet, an aquatic snail, which are made of the strongest known biological material on earth, tougher even than titanium. Nor as strong as the three-feet long incisors of a hippo which could bite right through a small boat. No, not that strong, but strong, nonetheless. Our molars can bear down with over 200lbs of pressure when they need to.

But our teeth are not indestructible. All those years of munching and crunching, nibbling, and gnawing, and chopping and grinding can wear away the outer layer of enamel and flatten the biting edges.

Exposure to acidic foods, such as citrus fruits and fizzy drinks, also weakens the enamel, setting our teeth up for more serious problems like cracks and breaks. These may then expose fragile pulp tissue at risk of irritation and inflammation and, because the nerves in the core of our teeth lose sensitivity as we age, the problem may be serious before we notice any pain.

Along with this, our gums will be receding as we get older, so that the soft tissue around the root of our teeth becomes less protected. That's where the saying 'long in the tooth' comes from: this receding of the gums in ageing horses makes it look as though their teeth are growing in length.

Receding gums cannot be reversed, but scaling can help to remove hardened plaque and infected gum tissue which builds up in the shallow trough between the base of the tooth and the exposed gumline. Gingivitis is the early stage of gum disease, when plaque and tartar cause irritation; periodontitis is a more severe stage, which can lead to receding gums, wobbly teeth, and deterioration of the jawbone. The shrinking of your gums also means an increased risk of dental cavities developing at the root of your teeth.

We also need to be on the lookout for a dry mouth. Saliva plays an important role in maintaining oral health, as well as supporting your sense of taste, and ability to chew and swallow. Dryness can cause bacteria to build up in your mouth more easily, leading to tooth decay, gum disease, and the horror of halitosis. You can moisten your mouth by sucking sugarless sweets, swilling water between your teeth, reducing alcohol and caffeine intake, and smoking less.

There is also mounting evidence of an association between the health of our mouths and that of the rest of our body. It's possible that bacteria from gum infection may travel throughout our bloodstream, triggering inflammation in organs and tissues in other parts of our body.

What can we do as we grow older to look after our teeth, and keep our mouths as fresh as a daisy?

Grannie Gwen thought she had she had the answer. One sunny afternoon in the late 1960s she went off to get the bus to the dentist. Smartly dressed as ever, with hair shampooed and set, she dabbed on some lipstick, collected her capacious handbag, smiled, and said goodbye. She never had the same smile again. A couple of hours later she returned. With no teeth. Not a single one.

The following week she made the same trip to collect her full set of dentures: her new, everlasting smile. Grannie Gwen didn't have dental problems, but like others at that time, she chose to have all her teeth removed to avoid discomfort in later life.

That option is still, of course, open to you.

Oh, you don't fancy that idea? Well, here's a selection box of seven bite-size pieces of guidance that may help instead:

The Truffle: Choosing a top toothbrush

With the selection of toothbrushes on the shelves seemingly expanding as fast as my waistline, it seems more difficult to make the right choice.

Think first about the bristles. If they're too hard and you're a little too over-enthusiastic, you could damage your gums, the surface of your teeth, or the enamel. A softer brush can be just as effective, especially as the bendiness of the bristles means they can remove bacteria and loosen plaque in nooks and crannies. In terms of size, the brush needs to fit comfortably in your mouth, in order to clean the surfaces of your teeth on the tongue side, as well as the cheek side.

Then there's the big electric vs manual toothbrush debate. For me there's no contest: the electric experience wins every time, especially as I have a little arthritis in my wrists. My mum likes to use both: electric to clean; manual to polish. If you haven't switched to electric yet, take a battery-operated brush for a test drive first and see if you're converted.

The Bonbon. Bidding your brush goodbye

In between uses, show your new brush some love by giving it a daily rinse and keeping it in the open, to discourage bacteria and mould from growing on it. Sadly, it won't stay looking good forever, and in three months or so, or when the bristles become frayed or discoloured, it'll be time to bid your brush a sad goodbye.

If you have a cold, cough, or persistent sore throat, though, be heartless and ditch it sooner – you don't want to re-infect yourself with any nasty germs that may be loitering among the bristles with bad intent.

The Fruit Pastille: Picking your paste

Your dentist will almost certainly advise you to use a toothpaste that contains fluoride, as it can inhibit plaque from sticking to your teeth, as well as strengthen your tooth enamel. If you're allergic, there are alternatives now available, as well as toothpastes that have no sodium laurel sulphate (SLS), a foaming agent which can be an irritant.

Otherwise, there's an immense range of other features to choose from. I use a de-sensitising paste in the morning and a whitening paste in the evening. If I have a bout of tooth sensitivity, I rub the toothpaste directly onto the affected tooth until it subsides.

I've also tried cleaning my teeth with turmeric. Despite it being a yellow dye, it is traditionally used to whiten teeth and has the bonus of helpful anti-bacterial properties. Unfortunately, however, the initial step of getting the turmeric power into my mouth proved to be a very untidy business, making more mess on the carpet than a visiting buffalo and dowager put together.

The Petit-Four: Brushing x 2 x 2

It takes just eight hours for food to start forming into plaque, so wielding your toothbrush once a day is not enough. Aim for twice a day, every day. Always. And forever.

Also, while it's tempting to freshen up your mouth just after you've eaten, it's better to hold off for fifteen or twenty minutes. That's because you'll have acid in your mouth from your meal and your saliva needs a little time to work on it first; whipping out your brush too soon may in fact assist the acid to erode your teeth. If you're in a rush to head out after your morning muesli, though, try rinsing water around your mouth to remove some of the acid first, then brush.

Brushing too quickly is tempting as, frankly, it can be a pretty tedious task. However, your twice-daily dental clean should be at least two minutes long. Fortunately, you'll find an abundance of songs of around that length, so select your soundtrack and brush along to the end.

The Toffee: Perfecting your toothy technique

If you're scrubbing up and down or side to side, now is the time to stop. Too much vim and vigour may be causing damage. With just a pea-sized amount of toothpaste, try cleaning with small circular, gentle motions.

Massage your teeth with your brush; imagine wiping the mist from a bathroom mirror, rather than scouring mould off the grout in your shower.

Hold your brush at a 45-degree angle while cleaning along the gum line and just under it. That's where those bendy bristles come in handy to remove bacteria and particles which get stuck there. Then use a rolling up-and-down motion to clean the other parts of your teeth, including the chewing surfaces.

Don't forget, as most of us do, the tongue side of each tooth. Sure, no one is going to see that side – oh, except your dentist, that is! So, open wide and angle your toothbrush toward the inner gum line to get that gleaming too.

The Humbug: Sticking your tongue out

Before you finish, squeeze out a little more toothpaste, and give your tongue a treat too. The bacteria that grow there are hard to remove with mouthwash alone, so brushing the whole tongue is needed, reaching as far into your mouth as is comfortable – you don't need to touch your tonsils.

The Parma Violet: Bossing the flossing

Flossing seems to be the component of dental care that most of us miss out. Yes, me too. It's awkward and uncomfortable, and my mouth can end up resembling the jowls of the Hound of the Baskervilles after snacking on a stray sheep.

But I know that, as effective as good tooth brushing can be, it won't remove all the bits of food debris stuck between my teeth.

If I promise to floss at least once a day, will you too?

> Life is short.
>
> Smile while you still have teeth
>
> Anon

5. Gut, Glorious Gut

Guts seem to crop up surprisingly often in everyday chit-chat. There are the self-explanatory references to the guts as the stomach, as in 'my guts hurt' or the 'greedy guts' insult, but then there are also the more oblique expressions. Take for example, 'I've had a gutful' meaning you're generally disgruntled, or references to a lack of courage as in 'I haven't got the guts', a loss of hope and happiness with 'I'm gutted', or useful intuition 'my gut told me'. Sometimes 'guts' can even encapsulate someone's entire being, as in 'I hate your guts'.

It seems we have traditionally attached more significance to our guts than simply in relation to our digestive system, and maybe there's something behind that. However, let's start by considering their pretty impressive food-processing role.

I've just treated myself to a rather tasty Dorset-baked biscuit for my elevenses: buttery, but with a bit of a crunch, and not too crumbly. But where is it now?

Having been chewed by my exemplary strong and healthy teeth, mashed up with saliva, and then swallowed, it has been pushed down my oesophagus and into my stomach where acid is breaking it down and killing any germs. It'll be sitting there with my morning muesli and copious cups of green tea for perhaps two or three hours and then embarking on a sixteen-foot journey through the coils of my small intestine throughout most of this afternoon. Here nutrients will be absorbed (I hope my biscuit may have had one or two?), and there will be plenty of bile and pancreatic juice washing around to help me with my digestion.

What remains of my biscuit will then head off into the large intestine – just five feet of bends to negotiate this time, over a more leisurely thirty-six hours – while water is absorbed. Whatever is left will become part of a perfectly-formed, biscuit-flecked poop, heading for the exit early tomorrow evening.

If you were paying close attention, you may be wondering how the large intestine earned its name when it's quite a bit shorter than the small intestine? That's because it's wider: about three inches wide compared to one inch. Yes, it does seem a little unfair.

Our bodies contain microorganisms in their trillions: a myriad of species of bacteria, viruses and fungi which are collectively called our microbiome. These microbes mostly live in our gastrointestinal tract, particularly the large intestine, and outnumber all the other cells in our body put together. We could consider our unique microbiome to be akin to an extra organ, one that weighs a little more than our brain and is needed for our survival.

Researchers are still discovering how important our communities of microbes are, and particularly having a healthy and diverse gut flora. As well as defending our bodies against toxins and harmful bacteria, it can have a significant influence on our digestion and metabolism, body weight, appetite, immune system, and even our mood.

Perhaps those idioms which link our guts to feeling brave, cheerful, or optimistic, or being confident about what our instincts tell us, are based in reality after all?

What can you do to boost the range of good bacteria in your body?

Well, the great news for us is the lifespan of a gut microbe is only about twenty minutes, meaning the makeup of your microbiome can be changed quickly by eating the foods that healthy bacteria thrive on. Admittedly this is not such great news for the longevity-impaired microbe.

Building up a healthy microbiome may take around six months, and then you'll need to keep up those new habits to maintain it.

Here are some ways you can give your gut an uplift:

- Choose food rich in prebiotics which will feed your gut bacteria. Some options are onions, garlic, leeks, tomatoes, artichokes, asparagus, more fibrous green veggies, legumes, and bananas (yay!)
- Also look out for berries, nuts, flaxseeds, olives, brassicas, coffee, and tea – especially green tea. These foods and drinks are polyphenols which are considered to be prebiotics but have additional antioxidant properties, meaning they may reduce inflammation in the gut
- Then include probiotic foodstuffs and drinks – those which contain friendly colonies of live microbes – in your diet, building up your portion sizes to avoid any digestive upset

  Some good choices are:

  - ✔ live, unsweetened yoghurt
  - ✔ kefir, a sour milk drink with five times as many microbes as yoghurt. The name may come from the Turkish word "keyif," which means feeling good after eating
  - ✔ raw milk cheeses, such as cheddar, cottage cheese, Gouda, and mozzarella. Although most types of cheese are fermented, not all of them contain probiotics, so check the label for live or active cultures
  - ✔ sauerkraut, which is finely cut, fermented cabbage that is rich in vitamins, minerals, and antioxidants
  - ✔ kimchi, a fermented spicy Korean side dish or relish made from garlic, cabbage, and chill
  - ✔ soybean-based products such as soy sauce, Indonesian tempeh, or Japanese miso and natto
  - ✔ kombucha: a fermented black or green tea drink.

- Avoid artificial sweeteners and processed foods as they can disrupt the metabolism of your microbes and reduce the diversity of your gut flora

- Give your microbes a rest by avoiding snacking and increasing intervals between meals

- Spend more time in the countryside and don't be shy about stroking animals. Apparently, those living in rural areas have more microbial diversity - as do people with pooches!

And now, it's BBA time!

That's the Beautiful Body Awards - and you are a contestant!

However, the orange tan, well-oiled legs, and fixed grin are entirely optional. Indeed, they are irrelevant.

What the BBA judges are interested in is the beauty of your body on the **inside**.

Who will be winning in the categories of Loveliest Liver, Most Wholesome Heart, and Super-Stunning Spleen?

Who will be crowned a champion with the Cutest Kidneys, an A* Amazing Appendix, and the Most Gorgeous of Gallbladders?

And make sure you tune in after the break to see contestants vie for the title of Perfect Pancreas, Alluring Lungs, and Divine Diaphragm!

Given the guidance above, devise a plan to secure your place on the podium, lift high the trophy, and be sprayed with celebratory kombucha for winning...

The Most Glorious Gut Award!

6. Taking the strain

For some women, a son or daughter's happy birthday celebration also marks the not-quite-so-happy anniversary of their acquiring a haemorrhoid or two in childbirth.

Straining in other ways, including when constipated, can also cause blood vessels to enlarge and balloon in the rectal area, and the likelihood of having a haemorrhoid at some time in your lifetime could be as high as fifty per cent.

There's some good news though. We can probably put to bed the old wives' tales that piles can be caused by sitting on cold pavements, perching on hot radiators, wearing short skirts, or just about anything else that your parents or teachers didn't approve of you doing.

When I was a student, my femur was snapped in a road accident. As dusk was falling one blowy, rainy Saturday, I toppled off the back of a moped and into the path of an oncoming car. Fortunately, it screeched to a halt, and I remember the driver walking over to me, exclaiming "Oh, it's a person!", just before I passed out.

I woke up in a geriatric ward, wearing a nightgown that tied up at the back. Fortunately for me, the doctor on duty had just come back from the USA where he had been trained to use a ground-breaking new approach to broken limbs: surgery to fit a plate and pins. The prospect of ten days on the ward and an impressive ten-inch scar was infinitely more attractive than staying in for six months of traction.

It was just as well I didn't need to be stuck in bed that long, as I could not deal with the indignity of sitting on a bedpan. Day after day I held back from using it, hoping that tomorrow I would, slow step by slow step, be able to reach the Shangri-La of the ladies' loo.

Day six dawned and, shortly after lunch, I finally made that successful shuffle. But my joy swiftly swung to shame, as I was wheeled back to my bed, doubled up in agony, after having to push the emergency cord and be rescued. The subsequent efficiently-administered double enema led to an excess of embarrassment that echoed around the ward late into the night. I didn't put my contact lenses in the next day, to avoid seeing how everyone was looking at me; I don't remember any comforting words of sympathy.

The damage I'd caused myself through my stubbornness in hospital, brought me to my knees, literally, several years later in Peru. For five days I hiked with a group through lush greenery to the world heritage site of Machu Picchu. Each night we set up camp to the backdrop of chirping insects, and a flimsy bit of canvas draped on poles around a newly dug hole to create a 'toilet tent'. Which I flatly refused to use.

On the penultimate hot and sweaty day, my jelly legs took me tottering over Dead Woman's Pass at 4,215m (13,828 ft). I was just behind Colin, the fittest member of our team - who had succumbed to oxygen sickness near the start and been placed rather unceremoniously on the back of a horse. Was I elated by my achievement in reaching this ridge, at the highest and most strenuous point of the Inca Trail? Just fleetingly, as a photo was taken; at that moment, the turmoil of my innards required my full attention.

The final morning arrived and, as dawn broke, we reached our spectacular destination. The sweeping views took in the Sacred Valley and Urubamba River, flanked by mountains, while llamas grazed contentedly in the ruins. which were empty of people. But my joy on arrival was fleeting. I could have contemplated why the Incas abandoned this magnificent site. I could have marvelled at how each stone was cut so precisely, and fitted so closely to its neighbours, that no mortar was needed to keep the walls standing, even in an earthquake. Instead, I had eyes only for the signpost to the loo and then stared at the back of a wooden cubicle door for a full forty-five minutes.

"Never again" was the oath I swore to myself, and it's one that I have almost kept for over thirty years.

As I can testify, constipation can be a cause of piles or create a flare-up or an existing problem, and getting older and having a more sedentary lifestyle can exacerbate this.

My personal preventative measure is five dried apricots every evening, ideally mixed with a few walnuts and brazils and a square of very dark chocolate. And whenever I have found myself facing a hospital stay, those activating apricots are the first thing I pack!

Drinking plenty of fluids is also vitally important, as well as eating lots of poop-softening fibre.

Easy ways to increase the amount in your diet as you grow older are:

- If you're having a takeaway, order a main dish only and add your own brown rice or quinoa. Heating half a pack in the microwave takes one minute
- Keep skins on potatoes when you mash or boil them
- Add chickpeas and lentils to salads, couscous, or rice dishes
- Sprinkle linseed or flax seeds in cold drinks or on your cereal
- Eat wholemeal bread, but check the wording on the packet: seeded, granary and multi-grain bread can look brown, healthy, and downright delicious, but may be white bread in a clever disguise. These cunning loaves have fooled me several times and now I always check the label.

My other 'bowel best friend' is Puer tea, which has a nutty taste. In Asia, it is also known as 'slimming tea', as they say it gathers up all the grease and fat inside and gets it moving. It works. Very well. My advice is to drink it when you have a safe haven nearby to run to.

How do we deal with any haemorrhoids we may already have? In the good old days of the family doctor who did the rounds, a nameless relative had theirs removed at our kitchen table.

Fortunately, we weren't eating at the time. The doctor declined the offer of tea and ginger nuts afterwards.

Nowadays there are more creams and other medical interventions to shrink piles and reduce discomfort. A lovely hot bath with Epsom salts may also help.

In addition, you could also use an ice pack wrapped in a towel. But don't be tempted to use an ice pick, without a towel, instead.

Check the NHS website for more information and don't be shy about going to see your doctor, especially if you are bleeding or in continual pain.

Here's one final suggestion, which hails from my hometown of Bristol. Ah, beautiful Bristol. Famous for its sherry, its ship-shape fashion, its suspension bridge - and a special scale.

The Bristol Stool Form Scale uses words such as lumpy, cracked, soft and watery to describe poop in an objective way. What could be easier than referring to the 1 to 7 rating when talking to your doctor, rather than trying to describe it in your own words?

You can even get a Bristol Scale tea towel so you can memorise the classifications while you are washing up.

As those of us who hail from Brizzle might say, "What a gert lush gift ideal."

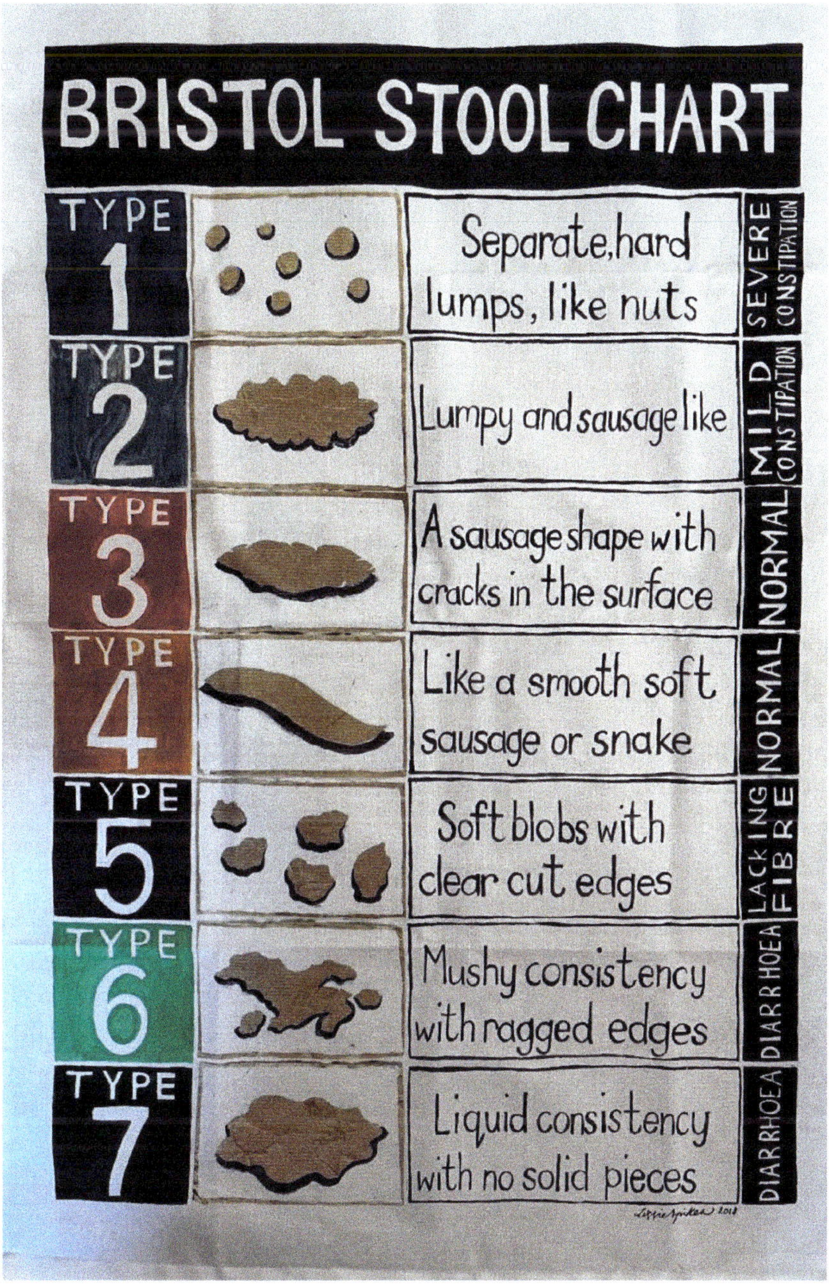

Designed by Lizzie Spikes in Aberystwyth for Driftwood Designs

7. Hi ho silver dining

> One cannot
> think well, love well, sleep well,
> if one has not dined well
>
> Virginia Woolf

Welcome to the Happy Silver Diner!

Come on in, take a well-upholstered seat, and have a look at today's menu, printed in an extra-large font.

Now, let me introduce you to Chef Silvian, who is going to take you through our delicious and nutritious options on offer today.

"Silver diners, we have here for you today a menu most delectable. Silver stomachs are not the easiest to please, but we have taken on the challenge!

"We have solved a conundrum even more vexatious than whether or not Miss Scarlett slunk into Dr Black's kitchen and hit him over the head with a handy bit of lead piping. What self-respecting chef would permit such an item to be among their pots and pans? Was it left beneath the sink by a sloppy plumber, with no consideration for health and safety, or for the highest standards of hygiene which must always be upheld? I assure you there are no such items in Chef Silvian's creative culinary space today!

Let us now focus on this conundrum we have cracked. Consider carefully what we know...

One, as we grow older, we start to become less active and so we need fewer calories to fuel our bodies. Otherwise, we will have waistlines that are forever and ever-expanding. Cal-horrific!

But, point two, at the same time as requiring a lower calorie intake, we need additional nutrients to keep our bodies working effectively. And so, my genial guests, to help you maintain bone health and density you'll need even more calcium and vitamin D than you did when you were wild young things!

"Plus, from the age of thirty, you have gradually been losing muscle mass and strength, in a process called sarcopenia. Eating more protein as you grow older may slow this rate muscle of loss, help your body recover better after illness, and keep you physically independent for longer.

"And now, my silver friends, we come to a further complication: point three. Just when we need these additional nutrients, our bodies become less able to absorb them. Our digestive system becomes less efficient at extracting the vitamins and minerals we need, and we particularly risk deficiencies in vitamins B12 and D, magnesium, calcium, and iron

"Let us dwell for a moment on Vitamin D, which helps your body absorb calcium. The cholesterol in your skin makes it when it is exposed to the right levels of sunlight. But that glorious sunshine becomes no longer enough! As your ageing skin becomes thinner, it also becomes less able to make the vitamin, so you'll need to find the right food as well, to ensure your levels are sufficient.

"We can also ponder how we can get additional protein if we are less proficient at processing it. As you reach seventy, consider spreading your intake of twenty-five to thirty grams evenly across the day. Yes, that does include breakfast too. But be warned, simply tucking into the tenderest of T-bone steaks won't help boost your protein levels as you won't be able to store all of it away.

"And so, my crinkly comrades, we come to point four. This is where we add a loss of appetite into the mixing bowl. The cause may be lower levels of hunger hormones, along with higher levels of fulness hormones, a diminished sense of taste and smell, dental problems, certain medications, and perhaps a general lack of motivation to make yourself a good, healthy meal, if you're eating alone.

"The dilemma then, for you silvery people, is that you need more protein, more vitamins, and more minerals! But, alas, you also need fewer calories, your body can't process nutrients as efficiently as it once did, and your appetite has deflated like a soggy souffle. What is a Chef to do?

"Voilà! I have prepared for you with passion and precision many petits plates. I have conjured a rainbow of fruits and vegetables, fish, lean meats and tofu, lentils, pulses and grains, nuts and seeds and set them in a forest of leafy greens: the tenderest trees of broccoli, the crunchiest of cabbages. the most succulent slices of cauliflower alongside the poppiest of peas. I have unleashed herbs and spices from around the globe to awaken your appetite and tingle your taste buds.

"Here's the Lovely Loreen Salad, packed full of green goodness, named in honour of Ms Dinwiddie who was the world's oldest vegan at 109. Or Noodles Okawa, named after 117-year-old Misao who attributed her long life to 'eating delicious things' – by which she meant sushi and seaweed, rather than chocolate and cake.

"Alternatively, you can build your own So Long Sarcopenia stir-fry, or sample our Happy Silver People signature dish: a banana and Marmite sandwich on our flatulence-free range of sourdough bread." He finishes with the flourish of a low bow.

Thank you so much, Chef Silvian, for sharing your culinary expertise. Would anyone like to ask a question? Yes, the gentleman at the back with the broad-bean-shaped head and the sherbet-coloured sweater. You'd like to know if there's an early bird special if you dine before five o'clock?

"Well, as you can see, Chef Silvian has left the room. He appears a bit eggy, frankly, and he's not mincing his words as he retreats to the pantry. Apologies for his spicy language. I can hear some crashing about and he's coming back with what appears to be some lead piping in his hands. Ah no, my mistake. He's wielding, with some menace, a frozen jumbo-sized vegan sausage roll.

I'm afraid the Happy Silver Diner will be closed for the next few days. In the meantime, perhaps you could sort out your own food shopping and cooking?

Your Eating-in-Colour Challenge

It's time for you to write a shopping list with a difference: one that is themed by colour.

Which foods are you going to select, so that you benefit from a rainbow of healthy and tasty goodies this week, and get the nutrients you need throughout the day?

Choose five natural and nutritious items for each. You get double marks for any items you've never tried before!

Greens	Blues & Purples
Reds & Pinks	**Yellows & Oranges**
Greys & Blacks	**Browns, Creams & Whites**

8. Shake up your drinks!

My formidable Great Auntie May lived in a converted cricket pavilion with Great Uncle Percy. It was pitched on a hill, not the obvious location for anything cricket-related, and had somehow been relocated from its natural home by crane.

GAM and GUP had no running water but fetched it from a pump across the field. Their loo was indoors, although somewhat basic. However, rather than spend time and energy upgrading her and Percy's facilities, she campaigned tirelessly for public WCs to be built in nearby Redcliffe Bay, right at the end of the bus line. The grand opening was covered by the local paper and attended by the mayor. What a legacy to leave behind!

GAM died in her late 90s, and I wonder if she spent the latter third of her life thinking about her own bladder, not just the bursting bladders of the waiting bus passengers she'd observed.

As I approach sixty, my bladder often seems to occupy my thoughts. I call her Brenda. She was a great friend to me in times gone by: so dependable on the very, very long train journey back to Bristol from York when I couldn't face using the loos onboard; so reliable on never-ending car journeys and long-haul flights; and during TV programmes in the days when you couldn't press pause when a 'comfort break' was needed.

Blessed Brenda. The kind of constant, uncomplaining companion anyone would want. Well, except for that one time when I simply couldn't miss the last thrilling moments of the Sooty and Sweep show.

But of late, Brenda has become rather high-maintenance. She demands immediate attention in meetings, or when walking down the street, or just as I am dozing off to sleep – and then also wakes me up in the middle of the night. Sometimes she gives up on me completely when I sneeze or cough. Or laugh. Or retch. Or just breathe.

Nowadays "Will there be loos or at least accessible bushes?" is the first question that pops into my head when planning to go out. It's hard to keep your sense of adventure when pleasing Brenda is the priority. Before the drive to my mum's house (potentially three hours), I have to calculate how much I can risk drinking beforehand, and by when I need to finish drinking to avoid needing to pee en route. Brenda is not the steadfast friend she once was.

So once again, there's tension brewing as we age. I need to stay hydrated, but Brenda is shrinking so isn't able to manage as much liquid, and her weakening muscles can't control the flow so well either.

Sadly, Brenda and I no longer agree on our favourite tipple. While my preference would be a gallon of green tea or a Happy Silver People banana-infused cocktail, hers is now simply water,

Why should water be my go-to choice as I age?

I suspect that this is what Brenda would tell me:

- Water makes up 60% of your body: 22% of your bones, 75% of your muscles, 75% of your precious brain, and 83% of your blood
- It takes nutrients and oxygen to your cells, regulates your temperature, helps convert food to energy, cushions your joints, and removes waste
- Your body loses water constantly, mostly through sweating and peeing
- As you grow older, the receptors in your brain may not detect changes in your hydration levels so well and, therefore, you may not feel thirsty when you should
- Your kidneys, which conserve water, may also not function as well as they did
- Being dehydrated has implications for your digestive system and dental hygiene and, long-term, may have implications for your absorption of medicines leading to a worsening of health conditions and increasing fatigue

- In severe cases, dehydration can also affect your memory and grip on reality. I am still haunted by visiting a friend's mild-mannered, snowy-haired uncle in hospital. He beckoned me over to the bed and asked in a whisper, "Have you seen one of these before?"'

  I wondered what he was going to show me. A treasured medal perhaps, an old coin, or a rare stamp that he had secreted somewhere in his hospital PJs? Sadly not. He popped his willy out and proceeded to wave it around with immense pride on his face.

  No, we didn't tell him about it when he recovered; he would have been mortified. It was a sobering lesson about what dehydration can do to you.

If, like my friend's uncle, you find drinking enough water a challenge, here are a few ways you might encourage yourself to drink more...

- Use a particular flask specifically for water so you can monitor how much you drink. Mine holds half a litre and I mix my prebiotic powder into it each morning for my first water intake of the day

- Drink your water through a straw. You should find you drink more and with increased frequency

- Think about the time of day you drink your water in order to maximise the benefits, and set an alarm to remind you. A suggested plan is:

  - ✔ two glasses after waking up to activate your organs
  - ✔ one glass thirty minutes before eating lunch and dinner to help stimulate your digestion
  - ✔ one glass with each of your meals
  - ✔ one glass before and after a bath or shower
  - ✔ one glass mid-evening to help you sleep but not wake up through the night!

Your mission

Design your own poster to encourage yourself to drink more water.

Already got this sussed for yourself? Then design it for a friend or relative to put on their fridge, or to go on display in your local doctor's surgery or on a work noticeboard.

Your second mission, should you wish to accept it

Water should be our number one best friend, not something to be shunned because society does not provide enough suitable and dignified places for us to pee.

Lobby for loos like Great Auntie May, and badger your local council for more Happy Silver WCs: well-located, accessible, clean, free - and open!

Don't forget to drink water and get some sun.

You're basically a house plant with more complicated emotions

PS Thanks to my surname, I am myself a Happy Silver WC. How I love seeing my initials on the front of so many doors when I visit public buildings, stately homes, and castles...

9. Weight on me

How grateful am I that our society seems to be becoming much more forgiving of the assorted and shapes of the human form. However, as I mentioned a few sections back, this year I resolved to lose 17lbs in 17 weeks.

Why? I was uncomfortable with my excess poundage. I felt puffed up and podgy. My clothes were tight and restrictive, and I looked forward to having a good old scratch of my keralus when I removed them at the end of the day.

There seemed to be more flesh outside my bra than in it, and in certain pairs of trousers, I appeared to have grown an extra pair of buttocks. When I moved, parts of my body echoed the movement for a few seconds, especially my underarms when I did something super-strenuous like wave my arm. Apart from my lower legs. They were no longer able to wobble, as they resembled wooden skittles which had been painted in an attractive shade of uncooked pastry.

In the past, I'd tried the highly anti-social raw cabbage diet, until my family begged me to stop. As I was only two days in, I can't comment on the efficacy of eating what was essentially coleslaw, but without the fun of the mayonnaise. There along came the Nimble bread and no-fat cottage cheese diet. It was just about sustainable for three weeks over one Easter break, although I didn't get to fly off like a bird in the sky at the end of it, as the advert had promised - not even in a hot air balloon,

In the run-up to my finals, I put myself on a strict calorie-controlled diet which I followed with determination for several months, along with my revision. My downfall was a visit to family friends in Portugal. Our hostess, Zita, baked fifteen types of cake for her daughter's birthday, held outdoors among the pine trees to the sound of chirruping cicadas. Of course, it would have been discourteous not to sample a slice of every single one. How did they taste? Todos deliciosos! Diet over.

Dieting is not a new thing. The Romans and Greeks, for example, were conscious of what they consumed from a physical and mental health perspective, with the Greek word diatia referring to a whole way of life. However, the idea of dieting for more aesthetic reasons came into fashion in the nineteenth century and became big business. Pills and potions were advertised to help speed up the metabolism, but they often had ingredients such as arsenic and strychnine which became additionally dangerous when dieters took additional doses to lose weight more quickly.

Lord Byron was one of the first celebrity dieters. He was conscious of his figure and popularised a diet based on vinegar, drinking it daily and eating rice and potatoes which had been soaked in it. This was supposed to cleanse and purge your body (as the unfortunate side effects were vomiting and diarrhoea) and to give the youth of the day Byron's fashionable pale and thin look.

If he were around today would his glossy book, *The Sour Taste of Sweet Success*, with a cover shot of him lounging against a stone balustrade, toasting the reader with a champagne flute of vinegar while the Mediterranean sparkles in the background, be tempting you as you wait at the supermarket checkout?

An even more extreme approach that gained popularity was the tapeworm diet. People queued up to swallow a pill containing beef tapeworm cysts in the expectation that the tapeworms would reach maturity in their intestines and absorb whatever they ate, causing the dieter to lose excess poundage.

Once the person had reached the desired weight, they then took an anti-parasitic pill to kill off the fattened tapeworm which might have grown to nine feet in length. Apart from the risk of abdominal and bowel complications in trying to expel the tapeworm, while alive it could also cause headaches, eye problems, meningitis, epilepsy, and dementia.

And then there was banting. A stout character in one of Agatha Christie's books of 1932, *The Thirteen Problems*, is described as 'banting', a method of dieting which dates back to 1862. It takes its name from an obese undertaker called William Banting, whose family business conducted the funeral arrangements for the Royal Household, including Queen Victoria and Prince Albert. It promoted the use of our fat stores as fuel for the body and a low-carb/high-fat approach.

Banting wrote about his weight-loss success in what is believed to be the first diet publication, a booklet called *Letter on Corpulence, Addressed to the Public*. He outlined the need for four meals per day, consisting of meat or fish with greens, with a piece of fruit as dessert, and dry wine to drink. Also emphasised was the importance of avoiding sugar and sweet foods, starch, beer, milk, and butter. Banting's pamphlet was so popular, and remained so for so long, that 'banting' came to be used to refer to dieting in general, and in Swedish banta is still the main verb for 'being on a diet'.

While we're at it, let's also recall the early twentieth century 'chew-chew diet'. This promoted the chewing of mouthfuls of food until all 'goodness' was extracted, then spitting out whatever was left. This was the brainchild of an American, Horace Fletcher, who became known as The Great Masticator and gained a phenomenal following, apparently including some well-known figures such as Sir Arthur Conan Doyle, Henry James, and Franz Kafka.

Fletcher provided guidelines as to how many times you had to chew certain foods, and dieters were timed during meals to ensure they had masticated adequately. It can't have done much for meal-time conviviality and conversation, or indeed for doing anything much during the day apart from prolonged 'eating': a single shallot needed to be chewed over seven-hundred times which could take ten minutes.

The evidence that you were a successful chew-chew dieter was determined by what came out at your other end. The goal was to produce 'digestive ash' just once a fortnight which Fletcher explained should be nearly odourless, with a faint aroma of 'warm biscuits'. In anticipation of questions, he considerately carried some round with him to illustrate the point.

I decided, without too much reluctance, to eschew all these tempting options for weight loss. Cutting out whole food groups was not going to work long-term for me and, while there was an undeniable attraction to having Hobnob-smelling poop, my real aim was to feel more comfortable in my body overall, and to adopt some healthier eating habits.

Did I succeed in my challenge? Well, yes and no. Over 17 weeks I lost 7lbs – and I kept it off. I also learned a lot from others who joined in with a similar challenge, and my new eating habits will help me shape up and shift more weight in the future.

That initial boost of losing 7lbs gave me the impetus to become more active, and also reduced my self-consciousness about how I might look during my initial attempts to get moving. I committed to walking to and from work each day (nearly four miles in all), having my first tennis lesson in fifty years, and trying out paddleboarding – all activities which will help me develop my strength, stamina, and suppleness.

By the way, in case you're fretting, let me reassure you that no tapeworms were harmed during my mini-transformation.

Now it's your turn to consider what you could do now to up-size, down-size or keep your current shape, in readiness for growing older

- Take a good look at yourself in a full-length mirror – front, back and sideways. Ask a friend to take a photo if you're struggling to see
- How do you feel about your shape and size overall?
- Are there particular areas of your body you would like to sculpt or strengthen, build up or bulk out, or maintain?
- What could you start doing now to help you move in the direction you want to go?
- Is there an initial target you can set yourself, which will then spur you on to do more?
- What's your plan? What will keep you on track?

10. The egg-tooth

The Big Yorkshire Silverback and I recently had a silver celebration: our twenty-fifth wedding anniversary. It was a joy to look through the photos of a quarter of a century ago, but it struck me that over a third of those lovely guests are no longer with us.

As we grow older, we'll inevitably be more exposed to sad news and events, such as the illnesses and deaths of family members, friends (of the human and non-human kind), colleagues, neighbours, and associates, and of the personalities and performers of our younger days.

Those who played lead roles, had walk-on parts, or made cameo appearances in our lives, will no longer be there. We may grieve for them all in different ways, and their cumulative loss may contribute to a feeling of detachment and even loneliness.

We may also have a changing perspective on negative news in the press and on social media. How will the economy, shifting world politics, and changes to the climate affect us as members of an ageing population, and as we are seemingly become less able to influence what goes on around us? How will different factors impact those who are dear to us and all those who will still be here after we've gone?

While we're looking at reasons to be not-so-cheerful, let's consider the frustrations we may experience: no longer being able to do what came so easily in the past; not looking as we once did; not making the same impression we might once have done; not being needed or sought out for advice and guidance in the same way.

All of this may be against a backdrop of being in pain or discomfort, feeling anxiety about finances, or facing the ongoing challenge of caring responsibilities, with the constraints and weariness that can come with them. It may be hard to spot a chink of sunshine at the end of the tunnel.

Coping with the curveballs life throws at us, and staying positive might be naturally easier for some people than others. Scientists are exploring whether genetics determine our own individual 'happiness level' to which we each default.

But for those of us who are not naturally predisposed to hit the high scores on the happy-ometer, and who may respond to the unwelcome twists and turns of life by retreating, the good news is that there are attitudes and behaviours which can affect how happy we are. And these are things we can do something about.

Let me take you back a couple of years, to when I was going through a challenging time. Again. It was a weekday and, as my alarm clock shrilled, my throat constricted, and my heart began to pound.

All I wanted to do was to burrow deeper below the covers, seeking to be undisturbed, undiscovered, and uninterrupted by the daily demands of life. I wanted to sidestep the pressure to go to work, to look after my daughter, to have to explain myself. I wanted to be awarded the freedom to sleep, and sleep, and sleep some more.

But it wasn't an option, and so began another day.

It's important we start practising our coping mechanisms sooner rather than later, so that we're more prepared to deal with the inevitable distresses of later life. This may entail consciously working to desist from dwelling on the negative, avoiding unhelpful emotional reactions, and abstaining from ostrich-like behaviour

I know that those times when I seek to build a thicker and thicker shell around myself are also the times that I actually should start tapping away at that shell from the inside.

Like a hatching chick, I need an egg tooth to create a crack of sunlight, and then break through completely.

My suggestion for anyone enveloped in a psychological shell is to make the smallest and simplest of steps to begin breaking out.

This might take some time, working fragment by fragment, and perhaps you may never break out completely. However, if you allow in enough light to function, and then a little more, you may start to feel more ready to embrace life again, and perhaps seek out more specific and expert guidance and support.

Here are some ways to start hatching:

- ✔ open the curtains or pull up the blinds to let in some real cracks of light, whatever weather the day may have in store
- ✔ tune in to a radio station that plays your kind of music. Sit back, enjoy their playlist, and listen to the live chat in between
- ✔ put on some fresh clothes you feel good about wearing
- ✔ make the space around you somewhere that you would choose to spend your time
- ✔ go outside, even for a few minutes, and take a look at what is around you
- ✔ talk to someone you get on with. It can be a very short chat but aim to ask them at least one question
- ✔ Get something - anything - in your diary that you'll look forward to.

Two years ago, the activity I chose to put into my diary was a haircut. I also decided I would act upon my New Year's resolution: to ditch the dark dye and embrace my natural colour, which I very much hoped would be a striking and sophisticated shade of silver.

What have I learned? That the time you most want to retreat from the world and create a shell around you is also the time you most need to reach out to the world and crack that shell.

Go on, get tapping!

Valuing others & the world around you

1. Kindness in five acts
2. A great attitude to gratitude
3. I just wrote to say...
4. The Man In The Hat
5. An own goal
6. Start it up
7. Starfish and snails
8. Going bananas
9. The legacy you leave behind
10. Holding on and letting go

Go to the Happy Silver People website if you'd like to download task sheets for this section

1. Kindness in five acts

Phew, we've reached the halfway point in this book! Three themes down and three to go.

I'm reminded of the evocative name of a stopping place in the Scottish Highlands: Rest and Be Thankful.

That's what we're going to do for a few sections. We'll be taking some time to reflect on ways we can value and appreciate others and the world around us, plus thinking about how, as we grow older, we can find new ways to contribute to our community and support others in small ways.

Perhaps a good place to start would be to consider how we can be kind. The word 'kind' comes from 'kin', as in 'family'. Let's not constrict our kindness, though; charity may begin at home, but it doesn't need to end there.

There are thousands of ways we can plan to show a little kindness, and bring a little joy or comfort to someone's day. You'll feel much better for doing it too!

Here are just a few suggestions to get you going on the downhill stretch :

- ✔ Next time you're at the till, give the cashier a mini box of chocolates to say thank you. (It would be even kinder if you paid for them first)

- ✔ Be complimentary. When you know you're going to run into someone, think ahead so you have a kind comment on the tip of your tongue: they're looking relaxed and well, the colour they are wearing today really suits them or seeing their smile has cheered you up

- Get fruity! When I was five or six, our next-door neighbour, Mrs. Butt, gave me a peach. She was widowed in her sixties and didn't have much money, but this was a treat for someone else that she could afford. And it truly was a peach of a peach. I can taste it now, and recall the sticky juice all down my arm. Even at that age, I knew Mrs. Butt had gone out of her way to show me a little kindness

  There are national days for just about any fruit and veg, and that means there are lots of great excuses for sharing carrots, mini-cucumbers, colourful tomatoes, and clementines with people you know. Eat a Peach Day? It's on 22nd August

- Sponsor a child, an animal, or a community, and then take up opportunities to contact them and get to know them better. Please be aware, though, that goats are notoriously poor letter writers

- When out shopping, buy a little extra and donate an item or two at the food bank collection point, or get some dog, cat, or hedgehog food for the local animal refuge

- Leave a book on a bench for someone else to enjoy. Check the weather first

- Make a Carton of Kindness. Fill a box with strips of paper with a selection of short uplifting sayings written on them, mixed with individually-wrapped sweets or chocolates. Invite your neighbours or colleagues to select a saying and a treat to brighten their day

- Make a call or send a card to someone you aren't that close to, but you have heard may be feeling a bit down or lonely

- Pass on a simple gift - a painted pebble, a packet of seeds, or a homemade bookmark (use stickers if, like me, you can't draw)

- ✔ Spread a few smiles – and set out to be a little more generous with them than you would usually be

- ✔ Leave a sticky note with a positive message on the fridge when you leave the house, a party, or the office.

But just before you head off to sprinkle a little kindness all around, consider what you're expecting in return. The person on the receiving end may be a bit taken aback and lost for words; the recipient of a card may never reply; and someone receiving a compliment may be a little embarrassed, or seem ungracious in their response.

Be prepared for a range of reactions (or apparent non-reactions), and simply trust that your gesture has made a positive difference in some way, even if you never know what it is.

I was brought up to be a polite little girl, so I imagine I remembered to thank Mrs. Butt for the juicy peach, but I doubt I said much else. I'd have liked her to know that I still remember her small act of kindness over half a century later.

> No act of kindness, no matter how small, is ever wasted
>
> Aesop

One other thing, don't forget to be on the lookout for opportunities to display some spontaneous kindness too.

I was surprised at how dependent I became when I was travelling while pregnant. I was working remotely in East Jerusalem, with the rest of the team based in London and Manchester. We connected by email for three weeks each month, and then I would fly back to the UK for a week packed full of meetings. This was 2003 and I don't think Zoom was even a twinkle in someone's eye.

On those trips, as I grew larger, I started finding myself having to ask strangers to help me carry or lift things, or to let me sit down.

After Lovely Laura was born and I went back to work, my UK visits were shifted to every six weeks. She would usually accompany me, and I sometimes struggled to manage her carry-seat, plus baggage, especially when I couldn't take her pushchair on board. I often had to rely on the kindness of strangers.

Roll on a year or two and we were back living in London. I would take Laura to hospital appointments in her pushchair. But the train platforms usually had no lifts, so there were flights of stairs to conquer, and even getting in and out of the carriage was difficult, unless you had the stride of a giant. Now I had to rely on strangers who were not only kind but had plenty of strength and stamina.

Fast forward again to me trying to manoeuvre a heavier Laura in a weighty wheelchair. Bus, train, and plane travel had all stopped for us by this time, but slopes, the shallowest of steps, thick gravel, and heavy doors that opened the 'wrong' way, continued to present a challenge.

In addition, Lovely Laura may appear to have two ordinary arms, but they seem to morph into a set of far-reaching tentacles at the least convenient times. How I would have loved some help when my little octopus lunged for the teapot in a café, pouring boiling water all over the table, or persistently pulled at the loaded tray I was balancing while simultaneously attempting to push her wheelchair towards a quiet corner, or she backed me up against a bookcase while trying to grab as many books as she could from the shelves, in a supermarket sweep all of her own.

'Would you like some help?' is an easy question to ask – and it gives the person being asked the option to accept gratefully, or decline politely.

The opportunities for random acts of kindness are all around us. There is even a day set aside for it, 17th February, when you can get some extra practice in. However, you don't need to wait until then, as a new week is just around the corner...

Which five planned acts of kindness could you carry out over the next week?

? What will you do to be kind to yourself?

? How will you be kind to friends and family?

? What kindness will you do in your local community?

? How will you touch a stranger with your kindness?

? How will you be kind to nature and the environment?

What was the outcome for each of your five acts?

Remember to be ready to apply a little **spontaneous kindness** too!

2. A great attitude to gratitude

What do you feel gratitude, appreciation, and thankfulness for right now? Yep, at this very moment?

Life will probably throw up some tricky challenges as we grow older, so it's extra important we are active about recognizing what we are grateful, appreciative, and thankful for – and that we show it.

I've found it helpful to break these three aspects down, and this is how I like to think about the trinity of indebtedness...

Gratitude

This is often driven more by the head than the heart. We sometimes need to remind ourselves of the multitude of things we should feel grateful for, as we tend to take them for granted.

A few excerpts from my list, in no particular order, are: not being in pain: being mobile; having a functioning brain; being part of a close family network and having kind neighbours; knowing there is food in the fridge; being able to drink the water from a tap in my own home; having an indoor loo; not being afraid to walk out of my front door; living somewhere with no earthquakes, extremes of heat or snakes, scorpions, spiders, or mosquitoes; being able to experience the rhythm of changing seasons and hours of daylight.

Why are some of these items on my gratitude list? Because I've experienced the opposite, such as debilitating toothache; sleeping out in the parks of Munich; living with water cuts, civil unrest and curfews in Algeria, along with a sizeable earthquake; being alert to the risk of bombings in East Jerusalem, especially when pulling up next to buses at traffic lights; experiencing the unforgiving heat of the desert; living on the Equator where darkness falls at the same time each evening; and being eaten alive by mosquitoes on an archaeological dig in Israel, from which I still bear the scars.

And my list will grow ever longer, as I learn more about the difficult experiences that others face.

Appreciation

This is what I feel for the myriad of people who make my life, and those of others, happier, healthier, and easier on so many levels.

I appreciate those who work in our health services and caring professions, and provide support through charities; who risk their lives when dealing with emergencies or going about their daily tasks; who empty our bins, treat our sewage, and bury our dead; who inspire and entertain us through their art, writing, poetry and performances; who come up with inventive ideas to solve problems; who lobby for justice and seek to find out what is going on in the world; who protect our countryside and keep it accessible to the public. I could go on; the list is long.

Thankfulness

My thanks go out to those people or groups who have helped in specific ways.

It's now noon, and I've just jotted down some thank-yous from this morning: to Reece who has fixed my washing machine and to Jan and Pat next door who let me use theirs when I got home from holiday yesterday; to my niece, Amy, for taking me paddleboarding while I was away, and to Alex who is bravely taking me on as a tennis beginner tomorrow. Also, reciprocal thanks to The Colour Works Foundation for the colourful 'Thank you' card and coaster which have just arrived in the post. No doubt there will be more to add to this list as the day goes on.

How can we get into good habits for showing a great attitude which will stay with us for life?

- **?** What's on your gratitude and appreciation lists? Can you add one item to both lists every day for the next week?

- **?** Who is on your thank you list for this week? How will you demonstrate your thanks?

3. I just wrote to say…

Our preferred time to tell the world how much someone means to us often seems to be when they die, rather than when they're still with us.

Hearing heartfelt orations and personal poems at a funeral, I sometimes wonder what the object of so much affection and admiration would have made of it all. I imagine their eyebrows raised in surprise at the words so carefully chosen by their close friends and family.

And if our nearest and dearest don't realise how much we appreciate them, what about the people who touch our lives for briefer periods, or more tangentially, and have no inkling of the positive impression they've made?

As I was growing up, I'd often be out, roaming around the village lanes and open green spaces with what would nowadays be called one of my 'besties'. Plus Bumble, of course: her black cocker spaniel who reluctantly provided the excuse for our excursions.

Mrs Grey was often out too, in practical apparel, bumping along a dark-framed wheelchair that held her grown-up daughter. Ellie had Down's Syndrome and her complexion suggested poor circulation. She would hold her hands in her lap, silently surveying the ground ahead on their long walks.

From the age of fourteen, my bestie and I were out pushing too, but in far less sensible clothing. Bumble now dragged his heels alongside a pram containing my baby brother, Hugh, who had the same condition as Ellie and matching florid cheeks.

Although we clearly now had something in common, Mrs. Grey and I never spoke. But I became aware that, day after day, year after year, hunched against sunshine, wind and rain, she quietly ploughed the uneven grass with an increasingly heavy wheelchair.

Years passed. Hugh was no longer with us, and Bumble was sniffing lampposts in doggie heaven. Then, by chance, I heard that Ellie too had sadly passed away in her forties. Mrs. Grey now had cancer and was not expected to live long.

By then I had a daughter of my own who had special needs and a wheelchair. I felt the urge to write to Mrs. Grey to let her know how much I admired her calm, her resilience, her fortitude. To say that I wished I'd spoken to her and Ellie all those years ago. To tell her that, when I was growing up, she had shown me how to get on with life, one day at a time, one foot in front of the other, because sometimes that's all you can do.

I kept finding reasons to delay writing that letter, though. I worried it might be intrusive, or sound strange, or I might be misunderstood. After all, I didn't actually *know* her.

And then it was too late.

Are there people in your life who don't know what a positive impact they have made on you?

If so, your task is to send them a letter or card to let them know. While you can.

Not sure how to start? How about something like this?

> Dear ______
>
> I was recently reading a rather splendid book called Happy Silver People.
>
> It suggested that we should write to someone who's touched our lives in a positive way, but perhaps they don't know it. This made me think of you!
>
> Do you remember...

4. The Man In The Hat

In those days I didn't know his name or anything of his history. None of us did. We simply called him The Man In The Hat.

He slipped into the tavern every day at half past one and took a seat at one of the small tables by the grimy window. His order was always a crusty meat pie and a single pint of ale, which he consumed alone and in silence.

He was a solid-looking man, neither tall nor short, with receding white hair, a neat moustache and narrow beard. His brows were heavy, giving him a severe look, but his eyes were kind and, on occasion, seemed full of sadness. I didn't learn the reason why until much, much later.

> The Man In The Hat always wore black, but in the fashion of twenty years earlier: his lapels too wide; his velvet waistcoat buttoned too high. Over his suit he wore a thick, dark coat which smelt of woodsmoke, and the sleeves hung long over his swollen knuckles.
>
> As for the hat itself, the wide brim was battered and frayed, and he would deliberately tip it forward, down over his forehead, as rose to depart. He left as unobtrusively as he had arrived, save for leaving a small tip on the bar and nodding politely to Mr. Watts, the landlord, on his way out.

A few years ago, I came across a new word, sonder. I discovered that it came from John Koenig's *Dictionary of Obscure Sorrows,* written in 2009. This creative work is full of words and concepts which Koenig felt should exist but didn't (until he filled that gap by coming up with them).

Here's the rather beautifully-written definition of sonder:

> The realisation that each random passer-by is living a life as vivid and complex as your own – populated with their own ambitions, friends, routines, worries and inherited craziness – an epic story that continues invisibly around you like an anthill sprawling deep underground, with elaborate passageways to thousands of other lives that you'll never know existed, in which you might appear only once, as an extra sipping coffee in the background, as a blur of traffic passing on the highway, as a lighted window at dusk.

Sonder gives an important reminder that those unknown people, who are the backdrop to each of our lives, have a unique life story, an individual experience of this moment in time, and personal hopes and fears for the future.

As we grow older there's a risk we become more set in our ways and our thinking. It may be particularly important to remind ourselves of the humanity of others, and also the walk-on parts we play in the lives of strangers.

Writing about The Man In The Hat is one way in which I can practise my awareness of sonder, without trying to make assumptions or stereotype.

Now it's your turn to practise...

- ? Which character in the following photos captures your interest?
- ? How would you describe their appearance and their movements?
- ? What kind of personality do you think they have?
- ? What are their feelings, their hopes, and fears?
- ? What might life have been like for this person?
- ? If they were a character in a book, what would ignite the interest of the reader?

Try a similar exercise with incidental figures in paintings or your own photographs

Do some people-watching (unobtrusively, but not creepily). Really look at passers-by and people who are in the background, and think about what kind of personalities they might have and the kind of lives they might live.

Remember, you're an incidental person in the background for them too!

5. An own goal

One of my favourite photos of myself was taken in 2018 when I was onstage during the family day for One World By The Sea.

I'd grabbed the mic to fill a little time while the stage was being set up between the Afro-Caribbean band and the Bulgarian dancers; a Cuban DJ was standing beside me at his mixing desk ready to step in if needed.

The bright colours of traditional costumes jumped out among the crowd (helping me to spot a local MP sitting between two flamboyantly-dressed flamenco dancers). and an appetising array of aromas filled the air, including sweet Thai pancakes, Goan curry, and Greek souvlaki on a spit.

I explained how the international festival had come into being the year before, going from an idea jotted down on a cardboard coaster to a three-day event, which we were then running for the second year. The previous days had included several didgeridoo workshops; hand drumming sessions, music and poetry performances, plus themed quizzes and food tasting for schoolchildren, students, and the public. Oh, and a super-impressive sambista band of drummers and dancers in full costume parading the streets in an explosion of noise and colour.

I felt we'd achieved our aim of celebrating the diversity of the town, providing a taste of other cultures to around 5000 people, and showing that we were a great location for international education,

On a personal level, I also gained a sense of satisfaction from working with a team from the International Education Association and securing funding from our town centre Business Improvement District, for both of which I then went on to become a Board member myself.

All this had enhanced my confidence, extended my knowledge of marketing and branding, and developed my skills in events management, begging people to volunteer as stewards, and negotiating with the occasional upset stallholder.

And I particularly got a lot of pleasure from building networks and collaborating with individuals from a range of different communities and groups which represent them.

Yes, I admit that the planning was sometimes maddening and could make me feel ill and, on occasion, I was resentful at giving over most of my respite time to it.

Overall, however, I'm not so surprised to learn that having a sense of purpose could be associated with a longer life, and one that is healthier and happier than might otherwise be the case.

The researchers* who came to this conclusion questioned seven thousand Americans aged over fifty. They defined purpose as being an intention which:

- is more far-reaching than day-to-day objectives
- is meaningful to you, but also of consequence to the world beyond yourself and
- involves progress, achievement, or completion.

Other Studies have suggested that when people see their work as connecting to a broader purpose and helping other people to achieve their goals, they are more satisfied with their careers.** Following on from that, satisfaction with your work, whether paid or voluntary, generally lifts your sense of well-being.

While pursuing people-centred goals seems more likely to bring us longer-term happiness, we can also differentiative between competitive goals and those which are cooperative. The first are goals where you want yourself or your team to do better compared to others, which means that you inevitably hope that the other person or group does less well.

Cooperative goals, however, lift up family, friends, neighbourhood, or a wider community, so that everyone can potentially do better or enjoy an improved experience. This means you can celebrate not only your individual success, but that of others too – bringing additional happiness.

If you've lived in Norway (sadly not something I've experienced yet myself), then you may have participated in a dugnad, a kind of community day when people come together to clean up their neighbourhoods by carrying out repairs, painting, or just having a clear-up – like a communal spring clean, but scheduled for all the turns of the seasons. As an enticement, I'm told there's kaffe og kaker (coffee and cakes) too. Where do I sign up?

The good news for all of us is that the stronger a sense of purpose we have, the stronger the positive effects on our brains may be as we age.

So, let's not have hobbies, but passions. Let's find a cooperative cause to propel ourselves forward. Let's get purposeful!

Could you...

- ? organise a dugnad
- ? be a befriending volunteer or support on the phone
- ? help out in a charity shop or refuge centre
- ? become a community driver
- ? chat to people, read a story, or run an activity in a care home, hospital, or hospice
- ? take dogs or cats for a walk, or foster them when their owners are no longer able to care for them full-time
- ? help backstage in a theatre, do admin for a community group, or assist in your local library
- ? litter pick in your local park or a communal area
- ? research an event or people significant to your local area, and then share your findings֍
- ? set up a book exchange in an unused phone box or bus shelter
- ? Or...?

֍ A fascinating example of this is the Remember Me project undertaken by Liz Ferguson of Hambrook, Bristol. She decided to 'get to know' the fifty-three soldiers of World War I who were listed on her local war memorial, and has shared her findings with the local community.

Which cooperative goal will you set yourself?

- What will you learn? Which skills will you develop?
- What will you personally find most challenging?
- What will your personal success look like?
- What do you hope to achieve for others?
- What difference will you make?
- How could you build on this as you grow older?

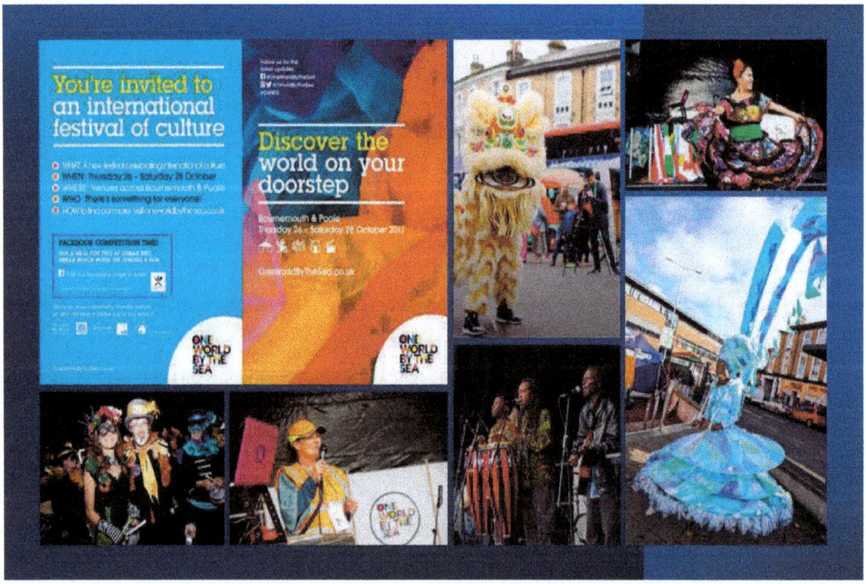

Images from the One World By The Sea 2017 & 2018
Including Barulho sambistas; Chinese Lion Dance by Dragon of the South; Colores Mexicanos; Afro-Tallawah reggae band; creative costume by Umoji. Photos by Zelda de Hollander, Sure Shotz. Thanks to the International Education Association for Bournemouth, Christchurch, and Poole

As you grow older,
you will discover that
you have two hands:
one for helping yourself,
the other for helping others

Maya Angelou

*Alimujiang, A., Weinsch, A., Boss, J., Fleisher, N.L., Mondul, A.M., McLean, K., Mukherjee, B., & Pierce, C.L. (2019). *'Association between life purpose and mortality among US adults older than 50 years.'* in *JAMA Network Open, 2(5)*

***Research on Work as a Calling...and How to Make It Matter*, Annual Review of Organizational Psychology and Organizational Behavior (annualreviews.org)

6. Start it up

I had what would once have been called a pipe dream; nowadays I guess we should call it a vape dream.

I used to imagine opening a café, one with beautiful geometric-patterned tiles on the floors, hand-woven rugs on the walls, and benches with embroidered cushions. Adjoining the eating area would be a covered courtyard with a fountain, where you could drink tea and coffee from a little glass, or smoke a fruit-flavoured shisha pipe.

One of the team would come round regularly to serve up pomegranate juice from a decorative silver urn on their back, or to swing a bucket of hot coals to replenish the pipes, and a white-robed whirling dervish or two might make an unannounced appearance and perform their mesmerising dance. Full health and safety risk assessments would have been completed beforehand, naturally.

On the menu would be little dishes of delicious Arabic-influenced salads, soups, dips, and desserts – akin to the 'mezze' of north Africa and the Eastern Mediterranean.

One of my inspirations was Algeria in the early 90s. There were no supermarkets, but there was some fabulous local produce on offer at the local market or souk. You could wander among stalls with bright fruit and shiny vegetables, grains and pulses of all shapes and sizes, sackfuls of fragrant spices and dried herbs, soft tangy cheeses, and huge black-market chunks of 'cheddar'. You'd see the freshest of fish, chickens, and eggs, as well as offal and camels' heads (neither destined for my shopping bag), and be distracted by the smell of warm flatbreads sold by ancient men in pristine white robes. You could even watch and wait while a new wooden spoon was made for you.

That was my dream for a business. Could it have worked? Maybe in the right location at the right time, with effective branding and promotion, food that was more than more-ish (and Moorish), and customer service that was worthy of praise. A robust and realistic business plan would have been handy too.

As a way of thinking about the local community, you're going to daydream about opening a business. However, you're going to approach it differently: the location is your starting point,

Here's some good news!

You've been given a commercial property on your nearest high street, and the funds to have it adapted (within reason), to run a business for a year.

Visit your high street.

Choose which of the empty premises you could imagine taking over.

The key question now is: what will you open?

Perhaps what's lacking in your high street is one of these:

- an insect restaurant called Crunchies
- a Big Foot, Little Foot shoe shop stocking extra-large and super-small sizes
- an Iron Lady laundry service
- a Twelve Months of Christmas store offering a year-round festive shopping experience, with Noddy Holder announcing "It's Chriiiistmas!" every time the door opens.

Start researching

- ? What makes your area distinct?
- ? What is the footfall at different times of the day and week
- ? What kind of people live, work and study in your area?
- ? What kind of people come to visit?
- ? What are the needs of each of these groups of people?
- ? What is available already to meet those needs?
- ? Could you do it differently or better?
- ? Or what is missing that you could provide?
- ? Could new people be attracted to travel to your area for this?

- ? Think of a brand and style for your business
- ? How will you promote it?
- ? How will make your service so good that your customers will come back for more, and recommend you to others?
- ? What will you look for in your team?
- ? Do you have a general idea of the likely cost of running your business from year two onwards? This could include typical rent, rates, supplies, staffing, taxes, licences etc.
- ? Are there any particular legal considerations you need to bear in mind?
- ? What could you do to make different aspects of your business more environmentally-friendly and sustainable?

Outline your business dream

You could add photos or drawings of how you imagine your business might look, plus a floor plan.

Share your ideas

Perhaps divide up the empty premises on your high street between yourself and some friends, and see how your different dreams come together for a revitalised area. Or all focus on the same property and have a competition to see who can come up with the most creative or viable idea.

What's the purpose of this task?

Who knows, someone may be inspired by your business dream and turn it into a reality.

If not, though, I hope it may help you to:

- understand your local community better, and appreciate the challenges and opportunities faced by local businesses and organisations
- see others' perspectives – their wants and needs - and re-consider your own now that you're getting older
- think about how you could contribute to supporting your local community: by volunteering, by setting up or joining a focus group, by lobbying for change based on the information you have found.

7. Starfish and snails

As the old man walked the beach at dawn,
he noticed a young girl
picking up starfish
and putting them into the sea.

He asked her why she was doing this.

Her answer was
that the stranded starfish
would die if they were left
until the morning sun.

"But the beach goes on for miles
and there are thousands of starfish,"
countered the old man.
"How can your effort
make any difference?"

The young girl looked at
the starfish in her hand
and placed it safely into the waves.

"It makes a difference to this one," she said.

Loren Eisley

My father loved the starfish story. He spent much of his life helping others, changing his life in his forties when my younger brother, Robert, was diagnosed with cancer at the age of eight. This was back in 1973, when you didn't hear about children getting cancer, treatment was often based on what was given to adults, and the survival rate was low.

We were fortunate in that we lived close to a large children's hospital, but my parents were struck by the situation of others with children undergoing cancer treatment who had to travel from further afield. These parents slept in hospital corridors, their families could be split up for weeks at a time, and some had to change their jobs to be able to take off the time they needed. The impact was significant; what could be done?

Mum and Dad opened the first home-from-home in the UK, where families could stay together, at no cost, and be close to their child during treatment. Dad then went on to found a charity with the support of many volunteers called CLIC (Cancer Leukaemia In Childhood) to offer accommodation and support to families across the UK, facilitate treatment, and fund research. The charity evolved into CLIC Sargent and is now named Young Lives vs Cancer.

Sadly, football-loving Robert died after fighting, and sometimes appearing to win, for four years.

Dad later went on to raise money for children with special needs and disabilities in memory of my youngest brother, Hugh, who was born with Down's Syndrome a year after Robert's death, and who died aged four from his heart condition. Dad worked tirelessly and creatively to help a wide range of charities and overall, it's been estimated that he was instrumental in raising more than £100m, making an impact on thousands of lives.

Dad was driven by wanting to make a difference to individuals. One young man from Portugal says that it was Dad's intervention which saved his life. Having undergone cancer treatment in Bristol when he was extremely sick, Pedro not only made a full recovery but remarkably went on to become a national swimming champion - in the butterfly category,

We may not be able to make such a significant difference, but we can brighten someone's day, and make little positive changes to the world around us.

I haven't had the opportunity to save any starfish yet, although I did once help some newly-hatched turtles into the sea in a nature reserve in Florida, Currently, I am on a mission to Save Our Snails. If I see one toiling its way across the pavement, likely to be squashed underfoot, I'll give it a helping hand to the other side.

What other small things can I do? Consistently provide water and food, such as succulent-looking mealworms, out for the birds – but not Marmite-y crusts, as salt may harm them; encourage bee- and butterfly-loving plants; keep lumps of dead wood in the garden as a home for our rather fierce-looking stag beetles; enable hedgehogs, foxes and the trio of badgers to wander by leaving a hole in the fence we share with our neighbours and lots of ground-level water to drink; remove rather than splat spiders who make their way indoors, or deter them with the smell of peppermint or eucalyptus.

You have just one question for this section, but it's a big one.

What's your plan for making a difference to one living being?

> We think too much
> and feel too little.
>
> More than machinery,
> we need humanity.
>
> More than cleverness,
> we need kindness and gentleness.
>
> Charlie Chaplin

8. Going Bananas

Ah! Bananas. You may have noticed one on the cover and one and on the back, plus a bunch of banana-flavoured mentions throughout the book.

Welcome to a little section dedicated just to them.

My love affair with bananas is quite recent and dates from when I recorded my first-ever YouTube video, all about yummy yellow foods. The banana seemed an obvious choice.

Why? For starters, the average banana contains around 112 calories and no fat. It carries a good contribution towards our daily dose of vitamin C, potassium, and magnesium which, along with its other nutrients such as vitamin B6, have been linked to improved sleep. Plus, it's full of soluble fibre which can promote better digestion.

What else? Well, a mashed banana could also work wonders as a face mask, mixed with honey and lemon (if you can resist the urge not to make pancakes instead), while rubbing the inside of the peel on your feet may soften and soothe them.

Alternatively, you can chop up the skins and add them to your compost, or place the small pieces around the base of your tomatoes, peppers, or flowering plants so they benefit from the potassium.

But never mind functionality, bananas should be loved for their radiant, joyous colour alone.

And for their curvy shape, of course, forming a ready-made smile to brighten anyone's day.

It seemed only natural to sign off from my first-ever YouTube video with a banana smile, an image that has stuck with me.

Inevitably, there is also a banana-themed back story to share, for Keren Bananarama and I have a few things in common.

Many, many years ago my dad and her mum went to the same church, and they even dated a couple of times.

Her mum went on to marry another lovely man with the same name as my dad, Bob Woodward

Keren and I went to the same Sunday School, but she was slightly older than me, and we didn't know each other. However, we did eventually meet, briefly, at a sixth-form disco on the outskirts of Bristol - at the school she and my bestie's boyfriend, Ian, attended.

Alan helpfully pointed out Keren and her friend Sara. They looked annoyingly alternative, confident - and fun.

"They're in a band," he said.

"They look a bit, um, tarty," I replied.

Yes, yes, I know. Even as I said it, I knew I was being a meanie. I was just a little envious that they looked much cooler than me. And they could sing too.

So instead of seizing the moment by casually saying, "Hi, our dads have the same name" and then following their stratospheric careers as a super fan, I went to the loo.

As I emerged from the cubicle, there were both Keren and Sara at the sinks. The following edifying exchange then took place.

"Ian says you think we look like tarts."

Good old Ian, I thought. Well, those weren't my exact thoughts, but I didn't have time to dwell on him as I only had a micro-second or two to summon up a sparkling riposte. I managed this,

"I think he must've misheard me. I said you look arty, not tarty."

And that was the end of the conversation. After giving me a well-deserved withering look, they left the WC.

My parents, however, stayed in touch with the 'other' Woodwards, and not so long ago went to Keren's mother's funeral.

"We had a nice chat to Keren," my mum told me afterwards. "She was there with one of those men from The Wham."

And no, she hadn't asked mum to pass on her best wishes to me.

What is your banana-tastic task?

- ✔ If you have a friend in need of cheer, relaxation, or a little roughage, offer them a banana.
- ✔ To put an instant smile on someone's face, give them a banana to hold up, so they can fake it till they make it.
- ✔ Failing that, pretend your bananas are microphones, put on Bananarama, and sing your hearts out.

> **Time flies like an arrow – but fruit flies like a banana**
>
> Sir Terry Wogan

9. The legacy you leave behind

A Romany fortune teller once told me I'd live into my eighties. I'm very happy with that prediction (and trying to forget she also told me I'd be very wealthy as, even looking through bionic binoculars, there's no sign of that).

However, for now, let's assume I'm fortunate enough to have another twenty-five(ish) years ahead of me before I pop off. Statistically, The Big Yorkshire Silverback is likely to have headed off into God's own country (no, not Yorkshire) already, and Lovely Laura won't be able to lend a hand with sorting through years of my accumulated 'stuff' – although I know she'd be super-helpful with shredding by hand or carrying out any tasks for which rapid de-assembly is required.

So I do need to be considering what can I do now to make it easier for whoever has to clear up after me in a couple of decades' time.

I think back to how I re-arranged my room as a teenager, so that it suited my changing needs and preferences – down came Donny and up went Bowie. Then later, as a student, my walls were adorned with album covers and art posters, and I acquired items such as a wooden hat stand, a sizeable stereo and more-sizeable speakers, an art deco tea set, and a 1960s wedding dress with white platform boots.

As the years went on many of these items were lost, broken, or discarded. Instead, there were collections of cassettes, videos, floppy disks, CDs, and DVDs, plus an ever-expanding bookery.

Travelling around the world also meant irresistible temptations to buy local pottery and glass, rugs and cushions, carvings and masks, even a marble-topped table or two (oh OK, there were three). Plus, more books. And so it has continued throughout my adult life.

But what kind of living space and contents will I be needing as I move into the next stages of my life?

And, thinking further ahead, what will happen to it all when I've gone?

Here are a few questions for you and me to ponder as we consider the longer term and a world without us in it.

Incredibly, without us here, the sun will still rise and set, the tides will still ebb and flow, and you can rest easy that there will still be a sofa on sale somewhere.

But what will happen to:

- ? where you live
- ? your dependents
- ? your pets
- ? your belongings?

Have you:

- ? made a will
- ? left details of your financial affairs
- ? set up power of attorney arrangements which can be activated when you can longer make decisions for yourself
- ? provided guidance about whether you would like to be buried or cremated; what kind of casket or ceremony you would like, or where your ashes could be scattered. If there are difficult family relationships, is there anyone you'd particularly like to be invited, or not invited, to your life celebration?

Is all this something those close to you may find it difficult to discuss?

They probably (hopefully!) won't want to contemplate a world without you in it. Perhaps you could, though, give them peace of mind by letting them know that you have thought this through, and where the information is being kept safe.

These are some BIG questions to think about, so let's limber up by doing a spot of light de-cluttering so that at least your belongings won't be too much of a burden – to your older self or to others.

Take time to consider:

? What do you need now? What makes you happy? What's superfluous?

? Where could you be living in the next few years? What might be your needs then? What may make you happy?

? What can you be fairly confident you'll be unlikely to need? Could you start with the full dinner service; CDs and DVDs; unused kitchen equipment; rusty garden implements; your childhood collections of china pigs, beer mats, or top trump cards; your old squash kit; clothes that are now the wrong size, style, and shape; bank statements from the 1980s? And maybe just a handful of books.

I like to use my tried and tested **KoDGeRS** method. For each item, this gives me only these options to select from:

Keep it - repair, re-purpose or retain it as it is
Donate it – where it can make a difference
Gift it - to a willing recipient! Perhaps ask for a photo showing your item in its new home in return
Recycle it - or its constituent parts where possible
Sell it – if you're sure it still has some value, and the effort is worth it.

Now let's identify the area you're going to focus on first and set a suitable timescale:

? Will you go for an achievable drawer, shelf, or box, or a more ambitious room, attic, or basement? It's your choice!

Just before you head off though, here's a poem I prepared earlier. I thought it might fit quite nicely in this section.

Toothbrush

If you read this, I will have passed.
Neither peacefully, nor raging,
but with a soft sigh of resignation.

I was not a blazing comet
lighting up others' lives with a wide smile or well-timed comment.
I did not win trophies or attract accolades,
rally the team, or leap to punch the air in triumph,
or donate my time or money until it hurt

No child will mourn for me,
seek the remnants of my scent.
in my favourite cardigan

There is no-one to stroke my gnarled knuckles
and recall the confident, swift movement of my hands,
as I knitted booties and blankets for the babies of others.

Who is left now to listen out for my laughter,
captured in the background of a wedding video,
or to spot me, caught unawares in a holiday snap,
eating fish and chips on a windswept beach?

A stranger will clear my freezer of fish fingers and vanilla ice cream,
will hold wide a bin bag for my rolled up tights and soft-top socks,
and will lift between their thumb and finger,
from the cloudy glass on the bathroom shelf,
my worn pink toothbrush.

10. Holding on and letting go

Question: What do these items have in common?

- a rusty blue tin flask
- a wooden metronome
- a string of pearls
- a shallow cereal bowl with rabbits around the rim
- a tiny English hymnal with scribbles on the cover
- a large, 50s-style, wooden dolls' house.

Answer: They are all items connected to people who have died and are still dear to me.

All these things would be firmly in my keep pile if I were applying the KoDGeRS method of de-cluttering. I can't dispose of them, but how can I ensure the memories attached to them will live on?

I'll be creating a memory bank with pictures of these items, plus information about the person connected to them and photos. Mine will be electronic files, but real folders could work just as well.

Here are some snippets from my work in progress. I've mixed up the extracts so they're not in the same order as the items, just to keep you on your toes.

- This was made for me, with loads of love, by Grandpa Cliff. He was kind and creative and could make and repair just about anything. He had an amazing shed dominated by a workbench and vice (which we would test out on our fingers), and an array of implements on hooks all around the walls. He was a tool maker at British Aerospace and to liven up one Friday afternoon, he let a flock of sheep into the workshop, causing havoc. Grandpa once had non-stop hiccups and had to stay in hospital for three weeks. We thought it might be a world record, but when we checked, it transpired he'd have needed to carry on hic-hic-hiccing for another 46 years.

- This is of value because it contains the only handwriting I can find of my brother, Robert. Scribbles like "I Rule OK" on the covers and inside pages could have been written by any schoolboy, including one who has terminal cancer and has lost his hair. I wonder what other notes in the margins he would have gone on to write as he grew older.

- These belonged to Nanny Beatrice. She had a tough life bringing up five children on a tight budget, especially after Grandfer became an invalid because of his TB. I was told that Dad and his siblings clubbed together to buy her something nice of her own. Nanny sometimes cooked us lamb chops on Sunday, and we picked the mint for the sauce fresh from her garden. Afterwards, we'd play hunt the thimble (with a high probability it was behind the chiming clock on the mantlepiece), and a game where we'd take it in turns to put our hands on top of each other's until we collapsed in laughing chaos.

- This was Granfer Cyril's. In the days before he was bedridden with a huge oxygen cylinder by his side, he worked for the AA. We have an old photo of him on a motorbike, ready to go out on patrol. He would have taken his tea and sandwiches (corned beef as a treat) for his lunch each day. For some reason, this is the only possession of his that we have left. I'm not sure how it survived.

- This was given to me by my Great Uncle Harry and Great Auntie Ivy who both loved music. They had no children of their own and wanted to encourage me to play the piano, as well as read a lot (especially the Brontës). Harry suffered badly from his diabetes and eventually lost his lower right leg, which was replaced with an actual wooden leg, highly polished and with a square hinged 'foot'. He spent years sitting in the same tattered armchair, smoking his pipe. When he died, Dad had their bungalow redecorated and brought in a smart new chair; Ivy made him go and retrieve the old one from the tip.

- This belonged to a little boy who gave big cuddles. When I was ready to leave for university in September 1982, I watched him happily playing with his red truck in the garden. He was so engrossed, I didn't want to disturb him. Hugh died suddenly three weeks later, so I never got to say goodbye.

Creating a memory bank as a way of recording the past will mean the recollections of people associated with these precious items will live on.

It also means I can let go of some additional items associated with these people, and with others. I will feel some regret, but also relief that what I feel is important has been retained. I know those who I wish to be remembered would not want their belongings to become burdensome to me, or to anyone else.

But then there is all the stuff that is related to me. Mementoes from my past which really don't have any value for anyone else now, and are unlikely to in the future, especially when I'm no longer here. Lovely Laura will not understand them, and there are no nieces or nephews on my side of the family to take an interest.

I've decided, therefore, to reduce the items from my past right down, capturing just the essence of the achievements that mean the most to me.

Instead of housing multiple items which hold similar memories, I'll save a representative sample. For example, to get started, I've found a picture frame with a mount that has ten little spaces.

Possible contenders to be featured include:

- One piece of text from a pile of uni books about Ancient and Mediaeval Hebrew, Aramaic, and New Testament Greek

- One sample of my Japanese homework from when I attended classes back in Singapore. When I first got my work back, I was alarmed to see the teacher had drawn a big red circle on it, but it was her way of showing I'd achieved 10/10. I now look at it agog, unable to believe I wrote it

- One snippet from a piece by Burgmüller that I remember practising and practising on the piano until I could proudly play it right

- An excerpt from my English Workbooks, dating back to my earliest days at school. This section is about the names of jobs. I've neatly written the right words under the nine pictures; eight of them show men at work, and one is of a woman. The waitress.

I can feel at peace throwing away the other items because I have retained a piece of them in my portfolio or memory box.

Now, what about thousands of photos covering sixty years of my life? Could I aim to retain half of them, and discard the others?

How about the stamp albums? The sets of replica army insignia which we avidly collected from petrol stations? Those elf ears?

Those will be interesting projects all of their own.

Your memento task

? What are you holding on to from other people? How could you record and share the memories that these items hold?

? What is it about you that you would like to remember later on in your life? What would you like others to remember about you after you're gone?

Which memories:

- ✔ do you need to be reminded of by an object?
- ✔ could be represented by an excerpt or a sample?
- ✔ could be captured in a photo of the item instead?

> **I often ask myself, will anyone I know be happier if I save this?**
>
> Margareta Magnusson

Enjoying & experiencing

1. Yes, yes, yes!
2. Rocking around your comfort zone
3. Kicks for free
4. Armchair traveller
5. Stepping back
6. Magic in the mundane
7. To define or not to define?
8. Life lines
9. Fade to grey
10. The lion, the witch, and their wardrobes

Go to the Happy Silver People website if you'd like to download task sheets for this section

1. Yes, yes, yes!

Stop what you're doing right now and pop on your pinny.

We're going to make a Yes, Yes, Yes Pie. No, it doesn't matter if you don't have an apron, just shrug on an old shirt over what you're wearing. Yes, I know you've got other stuff to do, but let's grab a few moments, and do this together. And yes, I'm sorry I didn't give you much notice, but we're both here now so can you forgive me and just go with the flow?

This is a super-easy three-ingredient pie. In fact, all we need are three lots of Yes, and you can add some pastry or crumble on top. Yes, mashed potato and grated cheese would make a great alternative. Sweet potato? Sounds delicious too.

Yes Number 1

First off into the mixing bowl, we'll pour a whole packet of powdered positivity. Don't worry about lumps, they'll just add to the texture and will give an extra burst of flavour.

In reality, there's not much in life which is 100% good or 100% bad, we maybe just need more practice at spotting the positive elements sometimes.

Happier people seem to naturally accentuate the positives, and minimise the negatives. However, I agree a relentlessly sunny attitude can become a little wearing, so we're simply going to aim for a general shift in the right direction.

Why is this necessary? Because looking on the bright side can bring some important benefits for your well-being. For example:

- you'll enjoy each moment as it happens because you'll be focusing on what's going right, not on what's displeasing you

- generally, our experience in real time shapes what we remember afterwards. This means that revelling in the better aspects of what is happening now will create a happier memory for you to re-play later on
- the more feel-good experiences you have, the more you'll want to seek out
- the less grumpy and grumbly you are, the more others will enjoy spending time with you – and, hopefully, you with them.

Yes Number 2

Now let's add a generous splash of optimism to our positivity. Even more generous than that. Don't worry about a measuring jug.

Around twenty years ago, the New England Centenarian Study got underway, with the findings highlighting certain characteristics of much older people. Among the attributes of those living long and living well (in contrast to those who were living long and 'dying well') were a positive mindset and less anxiety. Linked to this was an ability to look ahead to the future, as well as to deal with the events of the past, bringing with it a sense of happiness which could lead to lifespans being extended by four to ten years.

Perhaps another glug of optimism in our pie wouldn't go amiss.

Yes Number 3

Finally, we need to stir in an oversized dollop or two of forgiveness.

I remember a still summer's day when I was about fourteen, and standing alone and self-conscious as I waited for a friend outside her house. I watched as one of the older local boys cycled up the lane towards me but, inside of riding by, he stopped right in front of me. I was surprised he'd even registered my existence. Was he actually going to speak to me? Oh my goodness. Yes, he was!

"God, you're ugly" were his words. And then he pedalled away.

Well, it's only been 56 years that I've been replaying that moment in my head.

More recent examples include a snooty guest who took me to task at the dinner table for including some Boursin on the cheese board (luckily I wasn't sharing a circular cardboard box of Dairylea triangles as well): the online friend who consistently clicked 'like' on everyone else's Facebook comments, with the notable exception of mine; the troll who sent me a vile message (albeit demonstrating a creative use of expletives); and the well-known actor who berated a rather over-awed me at the 2012 Pride of Britain Awards for accidentally giving her a glimpse of my bra for a couple of seconds, as my silk dress slid out of place. I now know I must use double-sided tape in the unlikely event I get invited again. All of these incidents were minor but still left me feeling bewildered and embarrassed.

Over the course of our lives, people, even those close and dear to us, will be inconsiderate, selfish, or even deliberately hurtful in far more significant ways than my examples. I am hugely grateful that I haven't suffered harm or cruelty at the hands of someone else; the verbal bullying I experienced at one school was bad enough.

How helpful is it to hang on to unpleasant memories and to relive the feelings of shame, anger, or humiliation that they evoke?

Forgiving the person for their actions can help you forget the details of what was done to you in the first place, and this also means that all that the negativity associated with that person, time, place, and situation will not re-surface every time something jogs your memory. 'Forgive and forget' really can be a strongly- bonded couple.

Just because you've forgiven someone, it doesn't necessarily follow that you'll want to spend time with them or trust them again, of course, but they may stop influencing your mood or your outlook on life, and won't be haunting your thoughts at two o'clock in the morning.

So let me forgive and forget, and instead imagine inviting that uncouth youth to saddle up with me on a bicycle made for two.

You may have to forgive yourself a little too. I'd love to release other troublesome memories: the speech at a rugby club dinner which I'd imagined should be humorous and a little risqué but, I realised too late, was supposed to be a thought-provoking reflection on encouraging young people to take up sport. My thoughts were greeted with silence, save for the nervous titters of my friends.

Then there have been excruciating job interviews where I got flustered and fluffed the answers completely. Plus the countless times I've been thoughtless, angry, or impatient, or I've said things that were intended to be funny, but weren't. Ouch, ouch, ouch. How could I have said and done that?

How can I let it go, let it go? How can I rid myself of these miserable memories? I could write them down on scraps of paper and watch them flicker into flame and then curl up and burn, one by one. Or I could designate a pebble to each memory and then hurl them as hard as I can into the sea. Or I could chop up an éclair into creamy-chocolatey-chouxy bite-sized pieces, one for each negative memory, and then chew, chew, chew each one until they dissolve into the finest of purees. I think I could give that last one a try.

Let's have a very large slice of our Yes, Yes, Yes pie together and then commit to:

- Praising and thanking others, rather than finding fault
- Giving feedback which is not-so-positive in a constructive way, rather than simply complaining
- Opening our minds to opportunities and possibilities, even if our initial reaction may be to resist or focus on the pitfalls

- Thinking positively about ourselves and accepting we have sometimes been wrong, and will undoubtedly be wrong again. None of us can always be right
- Ridding ourselves of regrets and recollections which stir up negative feelings
- Dwelling on the positive in the present; finding things to look forward to in the future, and savouring memories of happy times in the past

Choose joy!

Don't wait for things to get easier,
simpler, better.

Life will always be complicated.

Learn to be happy
right now.

Otherwise, you'll
run out of time.

Anon

2. Rocking around your comfort zone

What do you imagine yourself doing with your time in older age? I'm seeing it as a wonderful opportunity for learning new skills and for brushing up on some of my rusty older ones.

I started to drive again in the UK in my mid-forties after not being behind the wheel for fourteen years, except once. My previous driving experience had mostly been on the other side of the road, and I'd never been the most confident of drivers. I recalled driving through France to Algeria, not looking the right way at a junction and hitting the side of a vehicle outside Marseilles. Luckily, it was an ambulance, and the crew could quickly ascertain there were no injuries.

However, I'd also driven down partially-completed motorways with bridge pillars suddenly coming into view, right in the middle of the fast lane; had negotiated potholes the size of Wales and the jarring ruts on the road surface caused by tanks as they'd rumbled into Algiers; and had willed our Fiat Uno up narrow, stony mountain tracks to reach remote Berber villages. I undoubtedly had some solid driving experience to draw on, but it wasn't until an instructor had guided me around Richmond Park at 10mph that I finally started to feel confident about driving again. It was something I'd believed would never happen.

Oh, the one exception I mentioned above? That was when I had the opportunity to practise some J-turns and other manoeuvres on the runway of an old airfield. Unfortunately, I lost control at one point and shot off the tarmac, taking the red STOP NOW sign with me.

More recently I've taken up paddleboarding as a way to relax, through being focused on the task in hand, responding to the movement of the water and the wind, feeling the warmth of the sun or the rhythm of the rain, and taking in the views from a fresh perspective. I'm also giving my core muscles some much-needed exercise, and am improving my balance. One day I'll even stand up.

I've also taken up tennis, with weekly lessons to start me off. I'm hoping to join the beginners' league in about a year. Don't tell me I'm too old to buy my first sports bra!

I've been a big believer in lifelong learning for many years, going to different universities in my twenties, thirties, and forties. It's too late for my fifties, but I won't rule it out for my sixties. But of course, learning doesn't just take place in an academic environment. There are opportunities all around us, we just need to grab them - and as I've grown older, I haven't minded so much about not being terribly good at something.

In the last couple of years, I've had a go at recording YouTube videos and have interviewed some fascinating people, I've been interviewed myself for a Podcast, spoken on local TV and radio, set up a website and, of course, drafted this book (albeit at the pace of an arthritic, but literate, sloth).

I've had some good examples to follow. Dad ran/walked his first marathon at sixty. It was the one in London and he carried three polystyrene children across his shoulders. It wasn't too aerodynamic when he was plodding uphill, but he made it through the rain to the end.

Then there was Mum. Over the years she made more pewter bookmarks than we had books; quilled paper scrolls on cards for every known occasion and then came up with new ones to celebrate (Happy Wednesday everyone!); was a hand-bell ringer and line-dancer (not simultaneously); volunteered in the WRVS hospital café and shop and helped run activities for people with brain injuries; was a classroom assistant at my brother's special school and, until recently, sang in the church choir.

During the Iraq invasion in the early '90s when it was feared many soldiers might be wounded, she offered to work in the Burns Unit if needed, and then signed Dad up for mortuary duty as, strangely, they hadn't had any other volunteers. He didn't respond too positively to the news.

You probably don't need to work in a mortuary to push yourself outside your comfort zone, but older age is not the time to stop. Instead, it's a crucial time to cast aside your scepticism and give new things a try.

Here are an initial twenty suggestions for activities you could consider in order to develop or refresh your skills, have some fun, and maybe meet new people too:

- Learn to use the camera on your phone more effectively
- Try karaoke. (Key question for me: can I actually sing?)
- Start using a spreadsheet to record your finances and keep detailed weekly, monthly, and annual plans
- Visit the local library
- Go along to one of the talks you see advertised in the library
- Improve your graphicacy – that's understanding and presenting info or data through images, diagrams and charts
- Learn to touch-type
- Set up an online escape room challenge
- Join a Knit and Natter group or get hooked on crochet
- Start swimming or go for a paddle
- Join a quiz team
- Crack some cryptic crosswords
- Write your own book or offer to read and critique someone else's book-in-the-making
- Buy a magazine about a hobby or interest you know little about
- Join a charity challenge: grow your moustache, dye your hair, wear a certain colour, do one hundred miles/laps/stairs in a timeframe that works for you, or go wing-walking
- Head off for a night away camping
- Join a fungi forage, preferably led by someone who knows their toadstools
- Cook beetroot and ensure it's edible before serving
- Boost your culinary skills by baking something from scratch: a cake, bread or your personalized pizza

- ✔ Sign up for a session or two with the U3A (University of the Third Age), or a weekend or evening class at a local college.

? When was the last time you did something for the first time?

? How will you get yourself out of your comfort zone in the next few months?

? Which new skills can you develop?

? Which rusty skills can you polish up?

? How can you continue to embrace the challenge of trying something new as you grow older?

It's time for you to write your list.

Life

loses its meaning

when we

get stuck

in the

comfort

zone

M. K. Soni

3. Kicks for free

It's pretty bad timing that many of us will need to be tightening our belts just as our waistlines are getting larger. I know that growing older will lead to my finances being squeezed, but it'll also encourage me to be more creative in my thinking and to appreciate all the fabulous freebies out there.

I can start getting used to a day or a week when I don't spend anything (except on bills), or a month when I limit myself to essentials only.

I can also be more resourceful about using what I already have. What treasures might I discover deep in the icy mists of my freezer, for example? And what other delights are already available to me at no cost at all?

I feel like bursting into song at the thought of my favourite (free) things ♬

For making life healthier

- ✔ videos about hiking and camping – they inspired the Big Yorkshire Silverback to get out and give it a go
- ✔ five tomatoes home-grown for the first time this summer
- ✔ ice cubes of freshly-cut herbs, pureed fruit, and pasta water (for cooking rather than plopping into drinks)
- ✔ healthy items for sale at a reduced price (almost free!) on their sell-by date for a spontaneous meal or to freeze
- ✔ the great outdoors – so many different environments in which to exercise, wander or simply sit
- ✔ parking further away, getting out the lift one floor earlier, or getting off the bus one stop sooner – and walking the rest
- ✔ flexing my muscles and testing my balance while waiting in queues or boiling the kettle
- ✔ apps with jigsaws and word challenges to stretch my brain.

For making life easier

- the Nearest Loo app
- phone reminders for just about everything
- my online shopping and holiday packing lists which I refer to again and again
- YouTube videos about how to change a plug, write a great speech. choose the right drill bit, sign a document electronically, darn a sock. cook beetroot...
- store cards which reward me with maximum points
- cash back through my bank when I buy from certain companies
- using my kitchen scissors, rather than a knife, to cut up pizza, salad leaves and anything that needs chopping.

For making life happier

- bird song and bird-watching apps. Did you know this is one of the fastest-growing hobbies among millennials?
- lying on the lawn to watch the stars
- amazing artwork coming into my inbox each day
- Eventbrite listings of multitude free events, webinars, and sessions, including some online
- a free bus pass - one day! Many bus company websites tell you what free events are on and how to get there
- the splendour of a sunrise or sunset
- 'behind the scenes' heritage and business open days
- libraries, libraries, libraries
- stand-up comedy or music in pubs and cafes
- being a film extra. This one's on my 'to try' list.

Of course, there's also the immense range of invaluable charity support on offer to provide free guidance and help when we face difficult situations. You might just need to ask.

How could you make your life a little easier, healthier, and happier – for free?

The best things in life
are free.

The second best
are very expensive.

Coco Chanel

4. Armchair traveller

Have you ever thought about the lines of latitude and longitude you live on? How are you inextricably linked to other places and people around the globe because of your location?

I'm currently in southern England at Latitude (east to west) 50.718395 and Longitude (north to south) -1.88337

Travelling due south down this line of longitude, I would travel through: Spain, Morocco, Algeria, Mali, Ghana, Burkina Faso, Côte d'Ivoire and, after a lot of swimming through the Atlantic and Southern Oceans, would cross Antarctica, then swim a little more through the Norwegian Sea, before hitting land again in the north of Scotland.

If I headed off to the east along this line of latitude I would come to: Belgium, France, Germany, Czech Republic, Poland, Ukraine*, Russia, Kazakhstan, Mongolia, and China and, after more strenuous swimming across the Pacific, would reach the shores of western Canada.

Those two long and rather dull-looking numbers are in fact the starting point for a fascinating expedition through a fabulously diverse collection of regions and seascapes – all linked to each other because of our geographical position!

Incredibly, it was back in the 3rd century BCE that a system of longitude and latitude was proposed. The proposer was Eratosthenes from Cyrene in Libya, who is also believed to be the first person to mathematically measure the size of the earth. In addition, he was an astronomer and poet, but most importantly, perhaps, he may have coined the word 'geography'.

Following on soon afterwards, Hipparchus, another Greek astronomer, was the first to use latitude and longitude as coordinates to specify location, suggesting that the zero meridian would pass through the island of Rhodes.

Over time, latitude came to be calculated quite easily, thanks to instruments such as accurate clocks and the sextant. To determine our latitude (in the northern hemisphere) all we need to do is to measure the elevation of the North Star, aka Polaris, above the horizon; when you move south, it appears closer to the horizon, whereas when you move north, it appears higher in the sky.

Alternatively, you could use the elevation of the sun at noon - a little trickier, though, as you can't look at it directly.

Measurement of longitude is, however, much more complicated, and the political, social, and economic implications of not being able to pinpoint locations and the distance between them became so great that the Longitude Act was passed by Queen Anne of Great Britain in 1714. The Act offered a £20,000 prize to whoever could produce a practical method of calculating longitude accurately while at sea.

The winner of the most reward money was John Harrison a self-educated English carpenter and clockmaker, who invented sea timekeepers and the first sea watch which could calculate longitude. Harrison was twenty-one years old when the Act was passed and received his reward forty-nine years later.

It's time for you to explore!

You won't need a sextant, sea clock, or strong sea legs for this expedition.

- ? Choose your starting point. It may be your birthplace, hometown, favourite holiday spot or a destination you dream of visiting; anywhere you choose!
- ? What are the lines of longitude and latitude? Which places do they pass through?

Now 'set sail' by starting to research your countries – maybe focus on a new one each week or month.

- ? What are people in this country doing when you get up, have lunch, and go to bed? What's the time difference?
- ? What would they traditionally be eating at each mealtime?
- ? Which languages do they speak? How do they say hello, goodbye, and thank you?
- ? How do they celebrate the arrival of a new baby, birthdays, and marriages? What other festivals and events do they mark? What are the rituals when someone dies?
- ? Which colours are culturally important? What is their national dress?
- ? What do they consider to be beautiful?
- ? What musical and dance traditions do they have? Who is the most popular singer or band now?
- ? Which animals or birds might you see in the wild?
- ? Who are their sporting superstars?
- ? Find out about three other significant people in this country, past or present
- ? What five fascinating facts can you discover?
- ? Find two images of the capital city, three of landmarks, and four of landscapes.
- ? What's the national dish? Can you make it or try new fruit or vegetable or drink from your chosen country? How about inviting friends around for a themed meal?

- If you exercise regularly, spend a day walking or running through the country – listen to the music as you go, think about the scenery or cityscapes you're passing, and the people you'd be meeting

- Find people there who share an interest with you: maybe other golfers in The Gambia, artists in Angola, jewellery makers in Japan, teachers in Tasmania, quilters in Canada, pianists in Portugal, magicians in Mexico, runners in Romania, urban gardeners in Uruguay, bee-keepers in Botswana, knitters in Norway, chocoholics in Kazakhstan, or cake lovers in Qatar.

- Next time you buy a book, choose one written by an author from that country or with a storyline that's based there.

For the stretches of water between countries along your connecting lines, you could also investigate the sea life and ocean floor.

Follow up by holding a Longitude and Latitude Day on 5 April.

Why that date? Longitude is from north to south, and both these compass points have 5 letters; latitude is east to west, and both of these have four. So, the fifth day of the fourth month seems apt.

Take the time to celebrate what you and others you will never meet have in common: a position on the globe.

I hope you enjoy exploring the world from your own home and that it will be good practice in being creative about alternative ways to have new experiences as you grow older.

*At the time I first wrote this section, I had no inkling of the imminent war in Ukraine. When doing this task, you may prefer to think of Ukraine as it was, and how, we hope, it will be again one day...

5. Stepping back

Let's take a rest from travelling geographically, and plonk down on the sofa. Let me know when you've breathed out the obligatory "oooooooph", slumped for a few seconds, and rubbed your feet.

Ready? Then let's go travelling through time. We'll be exploring the past, but this time we'll experience it differently

I've rented out a time machine and I'm going back to take you back with me to December 1993 for an unusual few days...

Wednesday 8 December.

Join me for a dinner at Guildhall, London in honour of Mr. Gorbachev. Yes, I do mean that Mr. Gorbachev. He's the president of only two charities, one of them being CLIC International, and Dad is on the host committee for his visit to the UK. The final day, Friday, will be spent in Bristol, at Dad's invitation.

Unsurprisingly, dinner, in these grand surroundings, is a formal affair. Here I am with Dad (in black tie) sipping pre-dinner drinks in a large room with high, decorative ceilings.

The huge doors at the end are now opening slowly to reveal Mrs. Thatcher and her entourage. She's making her way through the room, taking the time to speak to everyone. Now Dad is being presented to her and she's asking who I am. Introductions are made, and she's rather charming. I notice that she and I are the only ones clad in long velvet – I'm in black, while she is, of course, in navy blue. We have something in common.

And now we're moving to the dining room. We've been serenaded by the Band of the Blues and Royals, and now the Orchestra of the Grenadier Guards are striking up.

Interestingly, the menu is in neither English, nor Russian, but French: smoked salmon parcels and trout mousse; wild mushroom soup; roast lamb with green pepper and veggies of the season (I have the vegetarian version); and pears in liqueur. This is followed by coffee and mini-desserts, accompanied by a Chablis and what is described as a 'chocolate wine'.

There are speeches and toasts to follow, and Mr. Gorbachev is presented with the Winston Churchill Award. He and Dad give each other a quick bear hug when they meet up afterwards.

Do I have any photos of this momentous occasion? Just one. It's a quick snap of me outside in the drizzle, just before the dinner. With my eyes closed.

Thursday 9 December

I'm not celebrating Donny Osmond's birthday as I would have been once upon a time. Instead, I'm still in London, and today I'm at 11 Downing Street, as Dad is collecting a charity cheque for CLIC during the Handicapped Children's Christmas Party. I'm guessing the name has since changed.

The Aladdin-themed event is being hosted by the Chancellor of the Exchequer, The Rt. Hon. Kenneth Clarke M.P and his wife Gillian who has her hair coiled up in her customary bun. Norma Major from No. 10 has also popped around to lend a hand.

Against a backdrop of a huge bauble-laden tree and an impressive curving staircase, excited children are mingling, while parents keep watch and cautious waiters clutch silver trays of tea-time treats. There is also a smattering of celebrities.

Most visible - and annoyingly audible - is Mr. Blobby. In just two days, he'll be No. 1 in the UK charts; sadly, the following week's chart toppers, Take That, are nowhere to be seen. I am, however, about to meet three Nolans, one of them being from Bucks Fizz and the other two being from, well, The Nolans.

Looking back at the programme, I'm reminded that I've been rubbing shoulders with the members of Right Said Fred, plus a couple of Gladiators called Scorpio and Saracen, both dressed for combat.

I'm wearing a long, blue Laura Ashley frock, and carrying a black clutch bag of my mum's. Sadly, there's no space for my trusty old Canon camera in there.

Friday 10 December

Good morning! We're back home in Bristol and waiting on one of the two wind-blown platforms at Parkway station. It seems an unlikely spot for the last President of the USSR to be getting off a train. But he and Raisa are disembarking, both beaming and ready for introductions to Mum, James, and the rest of their entourage for the day. Mr. Gorbachev and Dad have a longer bear hug this time.

Then we're whisked off, through the sharp-elbowed crowd of photographers and reporters, and past a crowd of schoolchildren, waving flags and flowers. We're part of the cavalcade, escorted into central Bristol by police outriders and other security vehicles, with sirens blaring and lights blazing.

We arrive at CLIC House, a Georgian building converted into a home-from-home where families can stay at no cost while their children undergo cancer treatment nearby. There are children, parents, and staff to meet; a giant Christmas cracker to pull (revealing three children inside), speeches to be made, and a huge cake to cut. The throng of press and TV crews are beside themselves, and flashbulbs pop continuously.

Then we're off to the Great Hall of the University of Bristol, for a special degree congregation. There are more eloquent speeches as Mr. Gorbachev is presented to the Chancellor for the conferment of his honorary degree, and then we all rise to our feet to give him a standing ovation, followed by repeated cheers.

Before the sound has died away, we're whisked out with the real VIPs and being driven in a convoy to Lulsgate airport, where the Gorbachevs' private plane is waiting for them on the tarmac. We chat in the spacious, wood-paneled cabin, and I kiss them both goodbye. Mr. Gorbachev and Dad share another, even longer, bear hug. Then we're off, and they're off too.

Did we take any photos ourselves? Well, someone took one. It's of Mum and Dad looking windswept at the top of the aeroplane steps.

I've enjoyed re-living those few days, but now I'm going to re-play them and do things a little differently.

This time I'll carry a camera and ask people to join me in a new kind of photo called the 'selfie'. I'll taste all the food and savour the flavours; I'll sit back and enjoy the music and closely observe what's going on around me.

I'll welcome Mikhail and Raisa with some well-rehearsed phrases in Russian, and ask Margaret, aged sixty-eight, for her top tips on ageing well. I'll strike up conversations with the great, the good, and the ordinary (like me). I'll challenge Scorpio to an arm wrestle and sing Jingle Bells with Fred. I might also try to puncture Mr. Blobby with one of Mrs. Clarke's hairpins. Then I'll pop it in my pocket as a souvenir.

As you can see, over those three days I had some interesting experiences and opportunities. Yet now, thirty years on, my recollection of them is pretty limited. As I grow older, my memory of these and other events will fade further, so I'll practise my powers of recall and have fun filling in some gaps with my imagination.

I'll let you borrow the time machine now, as long as you promise to look after it. You can head off to re-visit a happy, interesting, or exciting time in your life.

- ? Which date are you putting in as your destination? Why?
- ? What can you see, hear, feel, smell, taste?
- ? What emotions do you feel?
- ? What struck you then and would you be interested in now?
- ? What tweaks will you make to enhance the experience?
- ? What photos are you going to take, and what mementoes will you be bringing back with you?

6. Magic in the mundane

One of the first things to be packed when heading off on a Woodward family holiday is a pristine tea towel. My mother's invariable response to drying-up cloths whenever we rent a cottage, is, "They need a good boil."

I have visions of her stirring a bubbling saucepan full of greying tea towels with an oversized pair of wooden laundry tongs, while the smell of bleach pinches my nostrils.

Mum pronounced the same verdict on my own cloths recently, so I accepted the inevitable and re-stocked. This time I chose tea towels illustrated with the most beautiful beetroots, others made of Baltic linen in every subtle shade imaginable, and another for the Big Yorkshire Silverback depicting the colour chart for his home county, which naturally includes hues called nesh, flat cap, cobbled streets, sweating buckets, teacake, and chuddy.*

I also bought the Bristol Stool Form chart tea towel I recommended earlier as a birthday gift for my brother. What better way to brighten up the chore of washing-up?

We all have mundane, day-to-day utensils in our kitchen. They have a particular job to do, but why shouldn't they also contribute towards putting us in a great frame of mind? It might be their colour, their design, or the memories we associate with them that bring a little joy.

My trident for spearing pickled onions once graced my mother-in-law's table and reminds me of happy times with her; an itsy-bitsy, teeny-weeny, silver mustard spoon never fails to make me smile; and I love the weight and shape of my chunky metal salad servers, with their cool, smooth, shiny handles.

* Find tea towels to treasure from RachelleWDesigns, BalticBloom, and LighthouseLnHaworth. All on Etsy.

Do you have a wonderful wooden spoon or a cheering cheese grater (apart from when it jams in the drawer)? Does your coffee grinder bring a grin to your face, or your potato masher remind you of a magic moment to two?

How could you get more enjoyment from the objects you use in day-to-day life?

This might be by:

- ✔ how they look
- ✔ how they feel
- ✔ how they evoke good memories

How else could you get into the habit of engineering opportunities to have some happy-making objects around you every day?

Perhaps:

- in the shed
- in your workspace
- under the stairs
- in the loo
- under the sink?

> Make the little things that bore you suddenly **thrill** you!
>
> Andy Warhol

7. Life lines

What would you think if you saw an older person looking like this?

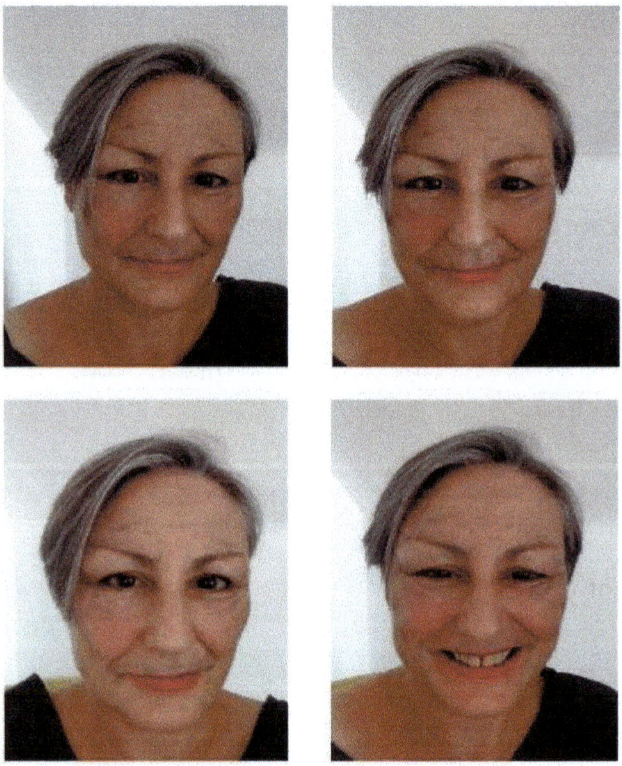

As I'm growing older, I'm naturally noticing more lines on my face. My skin tone and muscles are changing too, affecting the shape and contours.

Are these signs of my age something I should shy away from and hide? Is it possible I could come to accept them?

Is it even possible that I could embrace my lines? For example, by highlighting them with silver face paint, as shown in the photos.

Maybe one day our society will let us celebrate older age by encouraging us to draw attention to our lines, a bit like tribal scarring as a badge of honour.

In the meantime, though, I'm going to change the words I use about my lines. I can't imagine anyone thinking that having 'crow's feet' is an attractive proposition, although the Spanish reference to 'rooster's feet' is perhaps worse. I'd much prefer the Chinese description of 'fish tails' which conjures up flashes of silver on a sunlit river.

My lines are a life map. They tell the story of who I am, the places I've been, the people I've met and the experiences I've had. Some reflect happiness, some hardship.

There are crinkles which have been formed from a multitude of smiles and joyous moments. And then there are forehead furrows.

Mine have been exacerbated by frowning in difficult times, but that's not the end of the story. They also reflect years of focus and concentration in front of books and screens and, also thrown into the mix too, is the legacy of not wearing sunglasses when living in the glare of the hot sun. So, my vertical brow lines are not solely the product of negative emotions; they have been sculpted by good times too.

I cannot cease the creases. They are the day-to-day wear and tear of being a human being. I have them because my face expresses my emotions, rather than being set in stone. So, I'll try not to stress about them, or apologise for looking older.

I'm pleased that the beauty and fashion industries now feature more older women in their advertising campaigns, and they also appear increasingly often in the media. However, it's also noticeable that the mature women they choose to highlight tend to be the ones who don't look their age.

Somehow the perception of older men's looks is different; they are described as 'distinguished'. A little wrinkling and weathering can be attractive, as it's seen to represent wisdom and a life that's been well-lived. Wouldn't it be great if this response to an ageing face could be applied to women as well?

Your task for this section is a Dare, a Truth, a Kiss, and a Promise.

Yes, all four. No choices. But not in that order. Are you ready?

Truth

Rather than frowning at your reflection in our bathroom mirror, could you learn to accept the life lines on your face? At least some of them?

Kiss

Give your lined face a kiss in the mirror. It's the manifestation of the life you've lived so far, so what's not to love?

Promise

Commit to feeling more positive about your lines, not to feel self-conscious about them or to let them hold you back. Can you be crinkly and confident?

Dare

Emphasise your wrinkles with face paint or eyeliner. How do you look?

Double Dare

Could you now go outside wearing your face paint with pride, with your enhanced lines on show for the world to see?

I will if you will.

8. To define or not to define?

They say our eyes are the windows to our soul. In which case, are our eyebrows part of the window frame? They certainly have a functional role to play, but with my hair now silver and my skin tone lighter, it recently seemed to me the time had come for them to be given a decorative role all of their own.

The options were plentiful. Should I select the strong, regal brows of Cleopatra? Too contrived I decided, and milking all those asses for the associated beauty bathing was going to take too long after work.

How about 1940s-style pencil-thin arches, then? That was, perhaps, too haughty a look for someone hoping to radiate kindliness in older age.

Maybe I could try rocking a more natural, bushy look? This was evident in my wedding photos, where I appeared to have two shaggy black caterpillars crawling across my forehead. This would have been a natural fall-back position but since then my brows had become noticeably paler and thinner. Sadly, that meant I also had to rule out a statement monobrow.

Defining eyebrows has clearly become a thing in today's culture, in a way it never was when I was growing up. A compact mirror, sparkly blue eyeshadow, rose-pink lippie and dark red crème blush were the contents of my teenage make-up bag. But today there's an array of tools and implements dedicated solely to helping you achieve that perfect painted-on look for your brows.

It was time for me to start experimenting. And this is what I found:

- ✔ With my dark eye colour and the changing skin tone, brown was a much more flattering colour than harsher black. This was true for mascara and eye liner as well as brow definer

- To get a balanced look and the right proportions, I could line my brow pencil up with my nose, as the vertical centre point for my face. Holding my pencil in place at my chin, I could then swing the other end to the right, until it lined up with the corner of my mouth. The position of the pencil tip would show me where my right eyebrow should end. By doing the same on the left, I could create a fan shape which would emphasise the symmetry of my face. Apparently, that's a key factor when it comes to attractiveness

- Having defined eyebrows definitely brought my eyes to life – and helped to detract from the puffy pouches underneath

- The best choice for me was an eyebrow pencil which allowed me to make short, natural lines which didn't wear off too easily. It also had a spiral brush at the other end, so I was able to tidy through and remove any hard lines

- Defining with the help of a magnifying mirror and natural light was hugely beneficial, especially as those pesky stray hairs could be hard to spot

Brow definition is now part of my everyday routine, adding about one more minute to the usual five. And that eyebrow pencil is always in my make-up bag.

Strangely, the YouTube video I recorded about this got over 400 views; it's the most popular one I've made. I suspect trainee beauticians were being shown it as an example of how not to do a make-up demonstration.

It's time to decide. Do you define or not define? Do you pluck or leave bushy? Does the older you now suit a new shape?

Do you need to re-evaluate any other aspects of your make-up or daily facial routine as your face and skin change?

PS Just in case of any doubt, this section is for men too. Even the Big Yorkshire Silverback moisturises twice a day.

9. Fade to grey

What is it about our hair? We want it longer or shorter; wavier or straighter; in a natural cascade of curls or styled sharp and sleek. We'd like it a natural colour or dyed to look natural, or coloured in stand-out hues of the rainbow. Does anything change as we grow older?

There was a passion for perms during my early teens and I suffered from a few regrettable ones. These sadly did nothing to make me look like the wholesome, yet worldly-wise, model in the photo I'd carefully snipped from the latest Jackie magazine.

By my late teens, I was seeking a distinctive look but couldn't find it. Our local salon had a pungent smell – ammonia mixed with the fumes of the owners' collection of very hairy and malevolent cats. The matronly manager did not appear to know who Phil Oakey was, let alone how to re-create his distinctive half-long, half-short hairstyle on my head.

I tried elsewhere in vain and then moved on to the barbers. Could they at least give me a short back and sides? My plan was to then shave the right side of my head myself, back home in the bathroom with a Bic razor. They all refused.

My favourite haircuts would have to wait until Singapore in the mid-1980s. There the salon owner greeted me like a VIP. I would be placed in the window seat and a crowd would quickly gather outside to observe. The head stylist made a performance of his precision cutting and half-head shaving which was drawn out for maximum effect over several hours. In those distant days, before the age of Blockbusters videos, watching a strange English woman having a bizarre haircut made for great entertainment.

But let's go back to my nineteenth birthday. The day I had a blonde streak added to my fringe, at a time when that sort of thing just wasn't done. That streak stayed with me, on and off, for over twenty years. I found a way to DIY dye it of course, by using Jolen hair lightening creme. As it's really designed for facial hair, it's not too strong, and the consistency is easy to deal with (like clotted cream) so I could wrap my hair around my fingers a few strands at a time, and focus on the hairline rather than the more fragile tips.

From my late thirties, though, maintaining my blonde streak became more complicated, as the greys started to appear, and I felt the compulsion to obliterate them from sight. I felt I had to start dying my hair. It seemed my natural colour could be bought, packaged as a glamorous shade called 'medium brown'.

After a while, as the dye built up and darkened, it looked as though a dead crow was sitting on my head. I alternated full-head dying with touching up the roots on an increasingly regular basis, which helped to add different tones. Then the arrival of spray-on dye meant I could touch up those pesky roots in between the mini dye touch-ups, which were in between the full-blown dyes. I seemed to be faffing about with my hair colour every day by the time I reached fifty-eight.

"Time to stop this hare-brained behaviour," I cried. "This year I will make and keep a resolution!" That resolution was to embrace what I hoped would be my striking silvery-white locks.

To ameliorate the sight of lengthening roots growing out, I'd also have my hair cut very short as I started to reveal the natural me. And just think how much less damage I'd be doing to the environment if I stopped using those stinky chemically colourants.

My local hair salon started to strip out the colour and my first transformation was actually into a blonde. I rather enjoyed that – although I didn't get to find out if I'd have more fun, as the following week the pandemic struck. This interim stage ended up lasting around six months as all the salons were closed.

Then, after a hugely welcome haircut, it was on to stage two, where more brown dye was removed and, not so long afterwards, the coloured remnants had all grown out.

My hair is not the colour I imagined: I am surprised at how dark the back is, and that there is still an echo of natural brown. I like the way it mixes with streaks of silver, and ash and, well, grey. And I love my hair being much, much shorter.

The texture of my hair has also changed. It's no longer thin, fine, and fly-away, making it impossible to style; the coarseness of my greys now gives it more body than it's ever had before.

What have I learned about silver hair? That there is a risk it can develop harsh brassy tones. To counteract that and to enhance all the different tones of silver, I use platinum shampoos and conditioners. These have a touch of purple in them, that being the colour opposite yellow on the colour chart.

There are plenty to experiment with, including ones which have none of the usual nasties in them. I use the gentler ones two or three times a week, and the stronger ones (where gloves are recommended), perhaps once a month. If I spot a glint of lilac in my hair in the sunshine, I know it's time to lay off for a while.

But what about having no hair? My mum is convinced that almost every newsreader and weather presenter on TV is wearing what she calls a 'topper'. Could she be right? Would so many people go to such lengths to disguise their hair loss?

I can remember the good old days when older chaps had cringe-worthy comb-overs, but surely nowadays a shaved head is an attractive alternative?

Time to bring in a couple of guest speakers...

As I don't have any personal experience of hair loss, I've invited two experts to share theirs.

First up in the hot salon seat, tipped back at the basin, is supernatural thriller writer, Jaki Lewis-Thompson.

And after her, brightly lit by the spotlights above the wall mirrors, is my little brother, James Woodward.

My Hair Affair

I've never known what to do with my hair, oscillating between long and short, straight and permed, natural and coloured, according to the latest fashion.

I once went jet black, much to the amusement of my kids who told me I looked like Elvis. Not a good look for a middle-aged woman.

One problem I always had, though, was fine hair. Very fine - and sparse, let's not forget sparse. My scalp shone through, the light bouncing off it like a billiard ball. I wore scarves to avoid stares and comments like 'Isn't your hair thin?'. You can imagine what I felt like saying to those 'friends'.

Ironically, whilst still a teenager, I went through a period of wearing wigs. Hot sweaty things. Synthetic abominations that drove me mad. But as it was the fashion, I complied, knowing that at least my own lack of hair was disguised for a brief period.

All that changed just before Christmas 2019. My partner and I were preparing to go to Vienna. I had new clothes, new shoes, but what to do about my hair? By this time, I'd run the gauntlet of various 'treatments - follicle stimulation at a local 'hair clinic' (which cost me an arm and a leg); seeing a dermatologist, and a biopsy. All part of the battle to accept the inevitable: I have Scarring Alopecia, where the hair is lost, the follicle scars over, and a replacement hair is never produced.

Accepting the diagnosis was difficult. After all, I'd been told that a woman's hair is her crowning glory. At the hairdresser's, an uncomfortable young lady stood behind my chair, asking what I thought we ought to do to try and make my hair look thicker. (How the heck should I know, it's your field of expertise?). Something inside me snapped.

"'Shave it!" I said. She blanched. I giggled at the look on her face. It took several minutes for her to do as I asked.

Fast forward to Christmas night, sitting in a Viennese concert hall listening to a full orchestra playing Strauss waltzes. I'd brought a wig, despite my experiences with them. What a mistake! Sweat ran down my face as I got hotter and hotter. Never again. After that I tried irritating bandanas, slippery scarves and then said, "X&#*!! it"

Now I get my head shaved once a month, to keep the stubble in check. My partner is getting quite adept at it. We call it a 'Ripley cut' after Sigourney Weaver's character in Aliens. Yes, I get some stares, and a couple of people have asked me how the chemo is going. Talk about putting your foot in it. There have also been some delightful moments too. My youngest granddaughter loves to run her hands over my head, saying it feels like Velcro!

Recently, I was in Harrod's, walking along minding my own business, when a young woman, handing out cards for a hair salon, launched into her spiel - before clocking my bald bonce. She smiled sheepishly when I told her I really didn't need her services.

"'Oh," she stammered. 'But you have a perfectly shaped head for that cut. It really suits you." I chose to think she meant it.

There are worse things than a bald head. Much worse.

Hair Today, Gone Tomorrow

From the day I arrived in this world until I was running riot at three, I had no hair on my head. Finally. it grew. Blonde, then brown; far from flowing, but firmly on my head.

Then, like an 80s one-hit-wonder, it started to disappear. By 13, when puberty and hormones leave you self-conscious, I had thinning hair to add to my woes. I managed to stay positive and joked that my hair loss was “due to my high testosterone levels”.

My dad was actually more upset about this than me and took me to a hair treatment clinic in Bristol. The treatment to regrow hair back then was electric current through the scalp, massaging in of Monoxidil - tested on lab mice that made them hairy - and covering my head with stinking, black, cold tar for hours, twice a week. I was a teen and had better things to do, so I soon gave up and forgot the idea.

When I started university at 19, I joined the Ju Jitsu club and their techniques involved defending yourself from someone grabbing your hair. It was rather embarrassing when people walked away with a few strands of what was left of my hair so, after a year, I shaved it all off. Sadly, this look upset my parents as it reminded them of my late brother when he had chemotherapy. But there was no going back for me.

Fortunately, by this time it was the mid-90s and Andre Agassi took the plunge and also shaved his 'swede'. Quite a few people commented on me being his lookalike. I lived in America then and was even mistaken for him a couple of times!

Thankfully, I am fairly self-confident and this is helped by my large group of friends who make light of most situations. One of my best mates suggested I grew a 'Sponsored Sweep Over' for charity as it would be hilarious for them to watch my side hair grow. I said I'd stick with my number zero and just make a donation instead.

I'm at peace with my follicles but I understand how hair loss could upset someone. Nowadays a quick trip to Turkey will give you a new head of hair for a price. Another option is to get your scalp tattooed with a faint ink to make it look like there's stubble. As my shiny bonce seems to match my face, though, I'm sticking with what I've got.

And the silver lining is that I've saved a fortune in shampoo and barbers' bills over the last 30 years.

Where are you going with your hair as you grow older?
Do you have big decisions to make?
How will you start to formulate and carry out your plan?

10 The lion, the witch, and their wardrobes

When I was around fifteen years old and starting to chop my hair, I also developed a love for clothes. I mentioned in an earlier section the weird and wonderful outfits I used to wear.

Then as a student, I took part in what may have been the first-ever fashion show to feature during the St Andrews Festival. I wore creations made of netting and plastic; re-styled vintage treasures from the damp, crammed second-hand shops of Edinburgh's Stocksbridge; and an ensemble made of sacking. For that particular turn on the walkway, as I had broken my leg not so long before, I was carried on over the shoulder of a well-oiled friend in a loin cloth. Sadly, no prince was sitting in the audience that year to spot my potential as a future queen.

Over time, my go-to clothing colour became black. Cool, forgiving and terribly easy. Until, one day when I was in my thirties, some colleagues persuaded me to join them on a visit to the House of Colour.

"House of Gullible more like," I muttered under my breath as we went in for our group session.

Lizzy was first up in The Chair, positioned in front of a wall-sized mirror. Swatches of assorted colours were draped around her neck: it was like being asked to try out a selection of bibs at the dentist. We were asked to identify which colours suited her most.

"What utter guff," I thought to myself.

But then I could see it. Some colours made her look tired and pallid, while others undeniably brought out the colour of her eyes and give her a healthy glow.

When it was my turn, it was apparent that my best colours were olive green, orange, purple - and brown to match my eyes. Surely that last one was obvious. I was always complimenting people when they wore colours to match their eyes, yet, for some reason, I'd never thought to do it myself. Doh and double doh!

And so my clothes shopping habits were transformed. I searched the racks by shade first and foremost, rather than style. I had some successes, but as life became more complicated in my forties and I also needed larger sizes, it became more hit-and-miss.

My wardrobe had one much-needed boost after I won a very generous Boden voucher. How was I so lucky, lucky, lucky? Well, there was a monthly competition to ask their dog, Sprout, the most interesting question. My winning query was, "Do dogs say bow-bow or woof-woof?"

I think there may be a UK north-south divide on this one, with Bristolian me insisting on the former, while the Big Yorkshire Silverback opted for the latter. However, beyond the UK, dogs speak entirely different lingos: hau-hau in Poland, hab-hab in the Middle East, and guk-guk in Indonesia. And when Lovely Laura does a doggie impression it's arf-arf or sometimes a huge roar. Or occasionally a ribbit.

Naturally, I doggedly went through every item on the Boden website that autumn and was able to overhaul my look with tops, cardigans, dresses, and shirts in all the right colours.

Now, as I'm going into my sixties, I want to re-kindle my passion for fashion, after the sartorial semi-wilderness years of my forties and fifties. It's time to move on from catching sight of myself in the mirror and wondering who it is looking back at me.

I have different challenges to contend with now. My skin tone and hair colour have changed, my shape is now more top-heavy. and I'm more of a size 16+ than a 12 to 14. But, glad tidings! My hats still fit.

Another reason for rejoicing is that, not only do some of those colours from the days of House of Colour still suit me, but I've been able to extend my range to more tones of blue and greys and silvers than before. Shades that match my hair work well, as well as those that match my eyes.

When I started drafting this section, I thought about focusing on what we should and shouldn't wear as we grow older. Every day a barrage of alarming videos and social media posts come my way. Try these three for starters: *7 items of clothing which are making you look old and frumpy!*, *Never wear this unless you want to look like a senior!* or *These outfits are ageing you by 10 years!*

To save you from watching them (yes, I have succumbed to the temptation), here's a summary of what they will tell you...

- No elasticated waistbands
- No leggings, jeggings, or treggings
- No capri pants: they draw attention to the widest part of your calf
- No plastic or chunky sandals
- No big patterns if you have a larger frame
- No baggy tunics: everything must be belted or fitted at the waist.

The other points they raise will be current trends, like the length and width of trouser legs, whether or not you tuck your shirt in, and how long and puffy your sleeves should be. This is more a question of not looking bang up-to-date, rather than whether you look 'old' and past your sell-by date.

The host for these posts will invariably be in great shape and sometimes in their twenties or thirties. Yes, a cinched-in waist does look great on them, and I'm sure they'll find flat ballet pumps with thin soles and no support sufficiently comfortable. The guidance also tends to be aimed at oldies with a larger frame, rather than those who are more petite.

Some of the guidance is helpful, but older people can suffer enough already from a lack of confidence in how they (think they) look, and one impact of that can be that they feel less inclined to socialise.

Perhaps, instead, we can actively promote the trend away from body shaming and towards appreciating the different sizes, shapes and appearances that we humans have, especially as this diversity becomes more noticeable with age.

Could we reduce the time and energy we spend worrying about how others see us, instead of getting on and enjoying life? I remember my dad in his eighties longing to go for a paddle in the sea, but holding back because he was embarrassed about his white legs. However, as my mum loves to say on such occasions, "Who's going to stop a galloping horse to look at that?"

So here are a few guiding principles, which I hope can put us in the territory of being self-aware, rather than self-conscious, and keep those crazy horses galloping on by:

- ✔ Nothing stained, ripped, frayed, or faded
- ✔ Nothing so tight, it looks (and feels) uncomfortable
- ✔ If you are wondering whether it's time to throw it out, it's time to throw it out - or subject it to an imaginative refresh
- ✔ Avoid fabric so thin that everyone can see what may best be left unseen
- ✔ I've never found a compelling reason for anyone to show the top (or more) of their buttock cleavage
- ✔ Plain white T-shirts can be unforgiving, whatever your age
- ✔ Sew on buttons and tidy up threads and sagging hemlines
- ✔ Check what you look like from behind and the sides, as well as the front. You can use your photos from the Weight On Me section
- ✔ Black, scaly elbows can detract from the loveliest short-sleeved shirt
- ✔ Don't buy anything just for best. Life's too short to keep a garment you love stuck in the wardrobe. Wear it tomorrow!
- ✔ Sales provide a perfect opportunity to experiment with different styles and colours. When trying items on, sit down in the changing room. You can then see if they fit as well, and look as good, as they do when you're standing up
- ✔ I'm not yet convinced that socks and sandals are a match made in heaven.

Please note: the section above is not a man-free zone

Getting old is like climbing a mountain;
you get a little out of breath,
but the view is much better!

Ingrid Bergman

Re-energising & reconnecting

1. Walk this way
2. Strolls with a silver lining
3. Watching paint dry
4. Ask away
5. Really hearing something
6. Fun Boy 73
7. It's pecha kucha time!
8. Wipe that frown
9. YYYs
10. ZZZs

Go to the Happy Silver People website if you'd like to download task sheets for this section

1. Walk this way

You may have flicked through this book and wondered where the sections related to sporting action have tucked themselves away. You know, the pages where I encourage you to take a deep breath and plunge into a life of activity. The chapters with titles like:

- Starting To Snowboard In Your Seventies
- Exploring Everest at 88!
- Learn to Luge in Later Life
- Down the Zambezi - with Zimmer!
- Scuba Dive Into Your Second Century

Older people are certainly achieving some amazing feats. Just look at the National Senior Games which is held every two years for senior citizens in the United States. It's a multi-sport event, similar to the Summer Olympics, but focused on adults above the age of fifty. (Nope, that's not a typo. I did mean to write fifty!).

Maybe I'll cover these sporting attainments in a future publication: *Around the World with 80 Happy Silver People on Space Hoppers,* perhaps? But, for now, I'm looking at good old-fashioned walking, because we don't have to be athletic to be amazing, and a just little physical activity may make a significant difference to our well-being.

Is there a link between exercise and becoming a centenarian? Research indicates that there could well be a connection.

A study focussing on 100,000 American health professionals, scored them in five areas: not smoking, maintaining an appropriate body weight, drinking alcohol in moderation, exercising regularly, and eating healthily.

It found that those who were ticking four or five of the boxes at the age of fifty could not only expect to live ten years longer but spend that time in good health, compared to those who didn't tick any.

Some great news is that you don't need to do masses of exercise to get some benefit. Another study found that people who ran for four or five miles a week reduced their chance of a fatal heart attack by forty per cent.

But you don't have to run. There have also been several studies showing that regular long walks can bring real benefits, and even a little daily activity alongside some dietary changes will help.

Post-menopausal women like me may have reduced bone density (osteoporosis), and men's bones can also get more brittle with age. Exercise, along with diet and possibly also medication, can help us to strengthen our bones, making them less susceptible to stress fractures.

My extra secret silver ingredient is the Stretch and Clench method. As you walk, extend each stride a little further than you usually would, to work your muscles that bit more. While you're doing this, also hold in your stomach, stand tall, and squeeze your buttocks as hard as you can. Stretching and clenching as you pace, will give you a walk with a difference (that won't be too obvious to passers-by).

One further tip, which I picked up from a documentary about national silver treasure, Sir Bruce Forsyth, is to ensure you swing your arms as you stride. It helps to open the airways in your chest and improve your posture. And it's how younger people walk. Good gait, good gait!

You could also try Nordic walking. If you learn the right technique with your poles, you could increase your upper body usage, so you work harder, but walking gets easier – as recommended by The Big Yorkshire Silverback when striding through the peaks.

But if you can only spare around ten minutes for a walk, here's an A-Z walking routine to follow. You can do it indoors or out, on the grass or the carpet, barefoot or in a pair of sensible shoes (ask your feet for guidance). Adjust if you need to - and remember I'm not a doctor!

A-Z WALKING...

in the Air
with a Bounce
like a Chicken
Down
imaginary
stairs
like an Egyptian
Flat-footed
Gracefully
Hopscotch-style
on Ice
as if you're J-J-Jive-walking

with a Kangaroo spring in your step

Lethargically
in a Marching band
Nonchalantly
On sunshine
Purposefully
Quick, quick, slow
with Rhythm
in Slow motion
Tall: on tiptoes

hill
a
Up
Volcanic-style – hot feet!

this Way (freestyle)

Xtremely quietly
along the Yellow Brick Road
in a Zigzag.

And now go back to the start

2. Strolls with a silver lining

There's a fine misty drizzle in the air and the dull sky promises a repeat of the earlier downpour. As I reluctantly pull open the front door, the cold seeps into my bones and I catch a whiff of damp leaf mould. I wonder if I really need to go out for a walk; I know the answer is that I do. So, I set myself a challenge as an incentive: to photograph whatever I can find that is coloured silver.

I take my usual route around the park opposite, past the running track, tennis courts, bowling green and children's playground, across the open field, along various paths, and a stretch of pavement. As I walk, the clouds soften, and the sun breaks through.

What did I capture with the camera on my phone? I spotted two-tone tree bark, shining raindrops, and reflections in puddles. I noticed decorative lead on a church roof, intricately shaped into the form of trickling water. I looked at things I'd never really seen before and found beauty and interest in what might be considered mundane. I found I enjoyed my walk far more than usual, too!

The following day, I set Mum the same silver challenge. Now in her mid-eighties with a grumbling lower back, she sometimes needs a bit of cajoling to go out for a stroll. But, despite the heavy clouds and sharpening chill in the wind, with her body cocooned in a long, avalanche-proof coat, and her phone clutched in a mittened hand, she seemed keen to head out. Passing the village school, she ran into a woman who had recently moved into a cottage nearby.

Mum explained her mission, and her new neighbour offered to help, so they spent some time walking together across the green, taking snaps of silvery leaves and shiny car insignia along the way. Back home, thawing out with the aid of a pot of tea and a digestive biscuit, Mum heard a knock at the door. Her neighbour had come round with a silver plant pot she'd been given for Christmas. Would Mum like to photograph it for her collection?

The silver challenge had proved to be a conversation starter - and it then led to further discussions between Mum and me as we shared our pictures.

We've done some other challenges since. One had a pink focus. We chose that one when Mum 'confessed' it was her favourite colour, but she hadn't wanted to admit it as it seemed too girly for a grown-up. It led to some good-natured(ish) debate about the boundaries between pink, red and purple, and we explored some new places in our search, down among bushes and brambles, behind lurching old tombstones, and in the nooks and crannies of bowing stone walls.

On other days, I've also tried finding objects to spell out words, encountering some particular difficulties on one sunny summer afternoon in Dorset. The word I'd set myself was **KNOLL**, the name of the lovely gardens I was visiting. I found a water feature with Neptune, surrounded by lazing fish and dancing dragonflies, to represent N; a statuesque leafy oak for O; for the first L, there was lychnis rose campion, looking vibrant at the base of a slender silver birch, with the second L represented by a crescent of chopped logs piled up beside tall, wavy grasses.

But K presented a mega-problem. There were no kingfishers or kookaburras conveniently swooping through the cloudless sky; no kites with colourful strings being flown; no curious King Charles spaniels snuffling through the undergrowth. Eventually, I admitted defeat and plopped down on the grass to take a photo of my knees - although I did capture a magnificent silvery-brown eucalyptus shedding long strings of bark in the background.

What might my next challenge be? Perhaps triangles, circles, or stars; objects to spell out a 'happy birthday' or 'get well soon' message; spring yellows, summertime silvers, or autumnal oranges; or perhaps the initials of a friend who's feeling down, so they know I'm thinking about them.

Through these challenges, I re-discovered a love of taking photos. I also summoned up the courage to share my pictures with an online photography group - and got some positive feedback! And Mum and her neighbour, Harriet, have had lots more walks and digestives together - now accompanied by floppy-eared Flora, who enjoys a doggie biscuit or two.

So, what are the benefits of a silver-lining stroll?

- ✔ Giving yourself a reason to get out and walk
- ✔ Becoming more observant of the world around you
- ✔ Practising your photography skills
- ✔ Using your pictures as a way of connecting with others

Now it's time for you to go for walkies.

My silver-lining record card

The challenge I set myself:

Where I walked:

Five things I noticed and photographed:

-
-
-
-
-

How I've shared my pictures:

What happened as a result:

3. Watching paint dry

Growing older seems to erode some people's tolerance levels, and I'm hoping it's not my fate to become a curmudgeonly, crabby, cantankerous old crone.

I notice already how I struggle more with loud noises, children screaming, and experimental jazz (oh wait, perhaps no change there). Waiting for the phone to be answered by a human being, sitting in interminable traffic jams, and listening to people bellowing into their phones have all become increasingly irritating.

When did I become so less willing to go with the flow, why do I let situations outside my control bother me so much, and why is the number of people who don't behave exactly as I believe they should soaring?

I know my responses would likely be exacerbated by being tired or in pain, so what habits can I practise to help me quickly readjust my intolerance levels down from 11? What life-long strategies can I use to help me re-set to a sunnier mindset?

Let's think about the part of our day or week that we enjoy the least. Perhaps something that is so dull or irritating that watching paint dry seems an attractive alternative proposition?

Sometimes waiting for Lovely Laura to get off to sleep could feel like torture. It could go on for hours, with her fidgeting, giggling, and jerking herself awake. She'd be determined not to nod off. I'd have to sit beside the bed with no lights on, no phone screen to distract her, and no earphones which might let even a whisper of noise escape.

I would dream of watching paint dry. Oh, how restful that sounded, how peaceful, how undemanding. My mind would be able to just drift away...

Let's have a think about some of those negative words you or I might use to describe situations that rile us:

BORING ANNOYING
DREARY MUNDANE
TEDIOUS

Now, how about we look at them in a new way? Ta-da!

BORING ANNOYING
DREARY MUNDANE
TEDIOUS

They scrub up quite nicely, don't they? In fact, with a bit of a re-style and some colour, they look pretty amazing.

There are so many fun fonts, as well as countless colours, that you can mentally apply to unhelpful words to help you shift your mindset.

When you find yourself saying or thinking the word in exasperation, conjure up the re-fashioned version in your head instead. Somehow it takes the edge off the negativity.

Over to you...

- ? Which three chores or activities do you dread or avoid during the week?
- ? Allocate yourself **more** time to do these least favourite tasks, but add in an element of enjoyment to transform them into something you might even look forward to doing. For

example, do your ironing on the terrace in your swimwear while listening to music (probably best to check that the forecast is for a dry day first).

? Which negative words are you going to transform into something brighter and happier in your head? Can you picture the new versions?

And just in case you reach breaking point, here's a 60-second emergency SILVER refresh:

- Step back from the situation – physically, if you can; mentally, if not
- Inhale for three seconds, hold for three seconds, and exhale for six seconds. Repeat. Repeat again
- Loosen the muscles in your shoulders, then in your face
- Value something that went right today, however small it may have been
- Envision yourself in a situation where you feel relaxed and happy
- Rearrange your face into a SMILE – think banana!

> **The happiest people don't have the best of everything, they just make the best of everything**
>
> Anon

4. Ask away

Back in 1938, the Harvard Grant Study started to follow a group of men throughout their lives, from youth, through adulthood, to old age. It has gathered a mass of fascinating data about lifestyles, relationships, work, habits, and levels of satisfaction.

One of the findings has been that people who have closer social connections to their family, friends and community tend to be not only happier but also healthier - and they live for longer.

Overall, it seems that working to develop our relationships with others is one of the most important things we can do to become Happy Silver People in later life. For example, the reason widows go on to live longer than widowers is often attributed to women being more effective at maintaining social networks.

So, how can we re-invigorate old friendships, and develop new relationships as we grow older? How can we be engaging? What will we talk about?

Let's start by escaping the echo chamber where our thoughts, beliefs, and opinions are bounced back to us and entrenched through the media and people we surround ourselves with.

The obvious impact of this constant echo-echo-echoing of our views is that we assume our ideas and opinions must be correct. When we encounter perspectives which differ from our personal worldview (and those of our echo chamber), we can become incredulous, disconcerted, dismissive and angry, and more entrenched in the belief that alternative views are wrong.

Yes, it's natural to surround yourself with like-minded people, but if you do it exclusively, you risk being left behind or becoming narrow-minded, especially in older age.

How can we start digging our way out?

- Use a tool like Flipboard on your phone or laptop to curate your news feed. I began doing this during the time of turbulent American politics. Could I be sure I wasn't just seeking out the media outlets which confirmed my thinking? I started watching a range of news channels, including those from outside the UK to ensure I was more fully informed.

  Flipboard also exposes me to articles and insights I'm not expecting, and I love the random gems that can pop up. Today's little treats included: *Green bananas can reduce cancers by more than 50%, study shows; 56 recipes which start with a can of black beans* and *South African tour guide demonstrates how click sounds work in the Zulu language.*

- Find some Facebook groups to join to extend your knowledge or skills. I belong to groups interested in photography, local history, travel, weird and wonderful things, clouds, and octopuses – oh, and writing books, naturally.

- Read a different paper from usual – not to get you frothing at the mouth, but find something you agree with.

- Buy a magazine you wouldn't normally choose. Although maybe the Parking Review, Emu Today & Tomorrow, and PRO (Portable Restroom Operator) Magazine don't need to top your list.

So, having started re-igniting our curiosity in others and the world around us, we can move out of our echo chambers and into a stronger position to build good, warm relationships.

How else are we going to connect with people, especially ones on whom we can count, no matter what comes our way?

If you're worried you might be stuck for a topic of conversation, be prepared (literally) something to say first. Here's a quick-fire round to warm you up.

Choose one of each of these pairs and then explain your answer:

black or blue
sunrise or sunset
spring or autumn
left or right
lion or lamb
hot or cold
town or country
birds or bees
knife or fork
sugar or spice
up or down
song or dance
fruit or vegetables
moon or stars
the owl or the pussycat
Lennon or McCartney
Jason or Kylie

Now try arguing for the other choice in each pair.

Then work your way through these with your own answers:

- ? What's your favourite way to spend a free day?
- ? Describe a holiday which sticks in your memory
- ? Where would be next on your travel list, and why?
- ? What are your hobbies? How did you get into them?
- ? What was the last thing you read? Would you recommend it?
- ? Would you say you're more of an extrovert or an introvert?
- ? What's your favourite quote from a TV show, movie or book?
- ? Who was your first celebrity crush?
- ? What one thing can instantly make your day better?
- ? Which song always tempts you out on the dance floor?
- ? Explain one of your pet hates
- ? Ideally, how would you spend your next birthday?
- ? Have you ever disliked something, then changed your mind?

- ? What would you buy second, if you won big on the lottery?
- ? What was it like growing up as the youngest/oldest/middle/ only child?
- ? Which personality or physical traits do you share with your relatives?
- ? What's something your family would be surprised to learn about you?
- ? How did you your parents or grandparents meet?
- ? What has made you feel proud in the past year?
- ? What's the scariest thing you've ever done? Why did you do it?
- ? A genie grants you three wishes. What are they?
- ? Which famous historical person would you choose to spend the day with?
- ? What's the most unusual place you've fallen asleep?
- ? Which fictional character do you relate to most?
- ? What's the most ridiculous outfit you've ever worn?
- ? If you could have a mythical creature as a pet, which one would you pick?
- ? What's your favourite story about yourself?

Your turn to get the conversation started...

1. Now you know what your answers to these questions are, consider how you think those closest to you would answer each one.

2. Let's see if your predictions are right. Go and ask friends and family your questions. Their answers may surprise you, and yours may surprise them. Just like in the couple in the Pinã Colada song,

   After some practice, head off and try out a question or two with people you know less well. Can you spark a conversation – and keep it going?

5. Really hearing something

"Oh hello, there! Sorry, what was that? Oh, you're flitting your way in and out of the sections in this book, and you've just landed up here?

"Well, you're very welcome, but it might be more helpful if you take off again and wheel back around to the last section first. Great. We'll look forward to seeing you a bit later. Perhaps after tea. I might need a quick loo break before then too.

"Now, what was I saying? Oh, yes, about conversation being a two-way process.

"Yes, I think so too. The last section did help with the questions, but - just based on my own observations, you understand, no, not a scientific study – I reckon some people will get worse, or should I say *even* worse, over time at holding a conversation. You know, when people take turns to speak.

"I mean, don't you think getting older makes some people just talk and talk? Oblivious to the poor person listening to them who can't get a word in edgeways. Garrulous, that's the word. Don't hear it often nowadays, do you? Yes, some of them barely pause for breath, let alone stop to listen to what their captive audience has to say.

"You're wondering what I think might be the benefits of conversational turn-taking? Good question.

"Well, you know, passive hearing is a pretty effortless activity. But active listening. Now, that's really quite a challenge. You need some conscious effort and concentration for that. And to be interested of course.

"An old friend used to tell me that communication boils down to these three things. Yes, that's right, Brenda. Yes, that is what I call my bladder. No, I didn't name my bladder after her. No, I don't know if she had a weak bladder too. Anyway, the human Brenda used to say there were three things to be aware of.

"Firstly, there are the words. Yes, what the speaker is actually saying. Well, obviously this is important, but – and this is what interested me – this may account for just 7% of the impact of the message we want to get across. Just 7%. Fancy that.

"Now after the words, it's the music. Well, not real music of course. You wouldn't be carrying around a soundtrack to play when you're talking, Although, yes, you're right you could programme something on your phone. Perhaps Jive Talking or Talk Like An Egyptian. Walk? Are you sure? Well, maybe a recording of a siren would be better, then everyone would stop and take notice.

"So, this is about the music of what we say. That would be like the tone of your voice, for example, and the pitch. Preferably not too high and squeaky, like Pinky and Perky. And the pace or speed. Yes, the rhythm too. Then there's the volume, of course, and the strength of the message being shared. I mean the force you're using to make your point, which would show you feel passionate about something, wouldn't it? Or not. Absolutely.

"Yes, I think I'm good at doing this on the phone as well. I can hear if someone's upset or happy. Tony Blackburn on the radio with his smiley voice. Lovely.

"Well, let me just remember. I think all this music counts for about 38% of what you pick up on when you're having a chat.

"The third one? Oh yes, the third one. Well, this would be **dance.** No, not literally. Yes, I do remember Tony Blackburn took part in Dancing On Ice. It was a while ago though, wasn't it? No, I don't think he's been on Strictly. Not yet anyway.

"Where was I? Yes, words, music, and dance. Dance is all those things we can detect from the speaker's body language. Like gestures and how they're standing, and shoulders up or down. Yes,

I know I wave my hands around too much, but sometimes I feel strongly about something and off they go.

"What else would be included in dance? Facial expressions give away a lot, don't they? And when people's eyes aren't in tune with what they are saying. Non-verbal clues.

"Now, if we've had 7% of our message being communicated through our words and 38% through how we're saying it, then it must mean 55% of our message is picked up by what our body and face are doing. Glad my mental arithmetic hasn't deserted me just yet. Yes, 55% is a lot, isn't it?

"So, that's what people are noticing when we speak, and it's useful for us to consider if our words, music, and dance are all aligned. It can help us become really good listeners too, of course.

"How? Well, by paying close attention and picking up how the speaker truly feels about what they're saying. I mean, maybe we can pick up that something is troubling them, and check they are all right.

"Are you tired, by the way? I noticed you yawning a few times just now. And you're fidgeting a bit. Bad back? Touch of trapped wind? I've got some peppermints at the bottom of my bag. Bit hairy, but should be OK. No? Sure?

"Let's jot down some other benefits of being a great listener and then we can have a break. Before that other reader comes back from the last section. Yes, they did seem nice, didn't they? Oh, yes, I'll be ready for a bit of cake then. Beetroot meringue? Interesting.

"Where's my pen? Glasses? Oh yes, on my head. OK, ready. Let's put a title and summarise what we've covered before we add more. Just remind me what we said."

Benefits of being a good listener:

- You can pick up on clues about what the speaker really thinks and feels, and then follow up if needed and appropriate
- If people feel you're listening to them, they will share more, so you learn more
- They will also enjoy the experience of engaging with you, meaning they'll want to spend time with you in the future.
- If you're an active, empathetic listener, you'll become more skilled at maintaining conversations, and perhaps at getting them started too, meaning you can extend your pool of connections.

"Oh, very good. Yes, I got all that. Very succinct. Well done. Yes, I know there are a couple of typos, but I can fix those later. Super quickly then, for the next bit. Some top tips for being a leading listener. Go!"

How to listen well:

A. Pay attention! Focus on what's being said, not on something else. Don't let yourself be distracted by your phone or screen.

B. Engage. Reflect back what the person has been saying to show you're listening. Ask relevant questions if you need clarification - then let the speaker move on.

C. Abandon jaw jealousy. That's when you're not genuinely listening to the other person - because you're planning what **you** want to say next. This would suggest to the speaker that what you have to say is, in your opinion, more interesting, relevant, or correct, or that you're itching to direct the conversation elsewhere.

D. Ask for more. Encourage the speaker to elaborate on their point by asking questions or requesting they tell you more. People tend to like being invited to share their knowledge or views.

E. Don't give advice. If the speaker is talking about a problem, you're not there to suggest solutions, but to listen. Some people prefer to work things out themselves, and you may not understand the full picture. They may be simply wanting the opportunity to get something off their chest, or to try to articulate an issue, or to have a sympathetic audience. If you have a suggestion you feel you absolutely must share, ask first if the speaker would like to hear your ideas. If they wouldn't, then don't.

"We're done. Just in time. Let's take a break. Yes, I'd love to hear all about your neighbour's new doggo. Which reminds me, do you remember Tony Blackburn's dog Arnold on Junior Choice? Do you think he said bow-bow or woof-woof? I was just reading something about... Oh, no! I'm so sorry. Totally distracted. Now, tell me the name of the puppy and let me see a photo..."

It's time for you to tune in your ears...

- What do you need to work on now in order to become a better listener, with strong habits you can take into later life?

- What could you do to be more aware of your audience, so you avoid being a speaker who drones on for too long, without engaging in actual conversation?

- When could you actively practise your two-way conversation skills this week?

- Afterwards, review your performance and note what needs further work

- Then look out for an opportunity to initiate a conversation and keep it going for five minutes, Reflect on how it went. Can you increase your conversation length to ten minutes next time?

6. Fun boy 73

My mum, Judy, became a nursery nurse when she left school at fifteen. The experience of working in some challenging classrooms probably helped her develop the skills she also needed to organise parties for over-excited children in the days when these were hosted at home, and the food and entertainment were also pretty much all homemade.

A party bag consisted of an apple, a small pack of crayons and a little notebook with a spiral binding, a plastic party whistle, a squashed slice of cake encased in blue or green icing, and a couple of leftover fishpaste sandwiches, curling at the edges. If you were lucky.

I still have one of Mum's old books, *Party Games For Young Children* by the practical Jayne Grey. It cost three shillings and sixpence in 1963 and includes a treasury of birthday party activities. There are singing games like The Farmer Wants a Wife, In and Out The Dusty Windows, and Oranges and Lemons, which in those days always concluded with a forceful 'chopping off' of heads. As the book warns, "The last two lines will appeal to the bloodthirsty young members of the party."

Also featured are balloon games, musical games and, naturally, games with matchsticks. One such example is Mr. Walking Match, where each child is given a knife, a match, and a small cut-out figure of a man. Hopefully, there would be no bloodthirsty young guests at that particular party.

Can you imagine enjoying some of your childhood games and pastimes if you revisited them today? Could playing younger help us to feel younger?

Satchel Paige incredibly continued as a professional baseball player until the age of fifty-nine. He was often asked about his age, and once responded with a question of his own, "How old would you be, if you didn't know how old you were?"

What would your answer be? It may be that our subjective age, not our actual age, is a better predictor of our general health, ability to recall, physical strength and dexterity, and longevity.

It's time to have some fun doing activities you enjoyed as a child

Sing all the nursery rhymes you can remember
Drape a blanket between the sofa and armchair to make a den
Treat yourself to a Sherbet Dip Dab
Challenge a friend to a conker fight
Browse through your stamp collection
Camp in the garden – you don't have to stay out there all night
Splash around in a paddling pool or under the hose
Model some plasticine
Have a midnight feast
Try French skipping - or just skipping
Hula hoop
Jump around on a space hopper (orange is best!)
Be horsey and canter over some homemade jumps
Send a Slinky down the stairs
Play marbles
Design patterns with a Spirograph
Create a picture with stickers or Fuzzy Felt
Wear fancy dress, just because you can
Blow bubbles
Chalk out a hopscotch grid and use it
Do cats' cradle with some string, or make the Eiffel Tower
Create a miniature garden in a shallow bowl
Concoct some pink and white coconut ice
Try out a clapping game - *I'm a Bow-Legged Chicken*, anyone?
Indulge in some messy play with a sand tray
Make an origami 'fortune teller', with different options to help you decide what to do today
Sit on the swings (don't turf any kids off first, though)
Listen to the children's songs they used to play on Junior Choice
Construct an Airfix module
Go fly a kite

Add your own ideas to my list.

Then use *One Potato, Two Potato* to select which ones you do

Growing old is mandatory,
but growing up is
optional

Walt Disney

7. It's pecha kucha time!

Yay-haaaaay! It's pecha kucha time! I'll go get my party clothes on, plus a novelty pair of glasses. Wow, pecha kucha. It's a dance, right? Or a cocktail? Maybe a masked carnivale?

I'm so sorry. No, it's not. No music. Or food, Or drinks, either. Yes, I know, a pecha kucha does sound like quite a lot of fun, but, well, it's actually a type of presentation. No, no, please don't turn over the page. It will still be fun, but not in a music, food, and drink kind of way. You can join in with me. And you can wear your party clothes if you really want to.

Pecha kucha (petch-aa koo-cha) is a concept from Tokyo and means 'chit chat'. It's a concise way of getting your point or story across: you have twenty images or slides and twenty seconds to show and talk about each one. Yes, in total that means a mere four hundred seconds or just under seven minutes!

How will this help you in your quest to be a Happy Silver Person?

Well, it's a visual and concise way of sharing stories about yourself and the people, objects, activities, and events which interest you. This is a skill you can start developing now, and continue practising into old age as a means of connecting with others.

Ready?

I'll go first with one I happen to have prepared earlier. I am hoping to wow you, dear audience, with...

Well, wait and see!

What secret lies hidden beneath this disused churchyard in the small country town of Woodchester, situated in the Cotswolds? What could be the reason for a large sunken grassy area amongst the weathered tombstones?

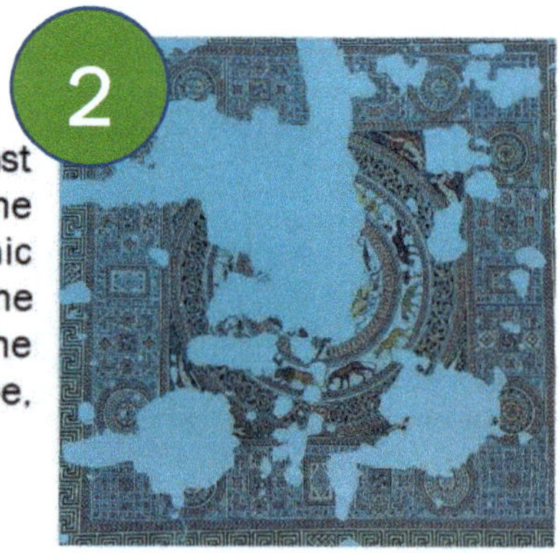

Six feet below the ground, and last uncovered in 1973, are the remains of the most magnificent Roman mosaic measuring 47 feet by 47 feet. It is the most elaborate Roman pavement in the UK, and the largest mosaic in Europe, north of the Alps.

The last time it was revealed, only 60% of the mosaic remained. It had been damaged by the elements when previously uncovered, as well as by unsuspecting gravediggers in the more distant past. The first known reference to it dates from 1695, but it was Samuel Lysons in 1796 who drew and described it in detail, following his own four-year excavation of the site.

Lysons named the mosaic The Great Pavement, and recorded that it told the story of Orpheus, the musician in Greek mythology whose music charmed the birds and beasts from sky, land, and sea. Given the scale and skilful design of the mosaic, this was probably the dining room floor of the villa of the Governor of this part of Roman Britain in 325 CE: a wall-to-wall stone carpet designed to impress!

The uncovering of the mosaic for two weeks in 1973 brought such disruption to Woodchester that seemed unlikely the mosaic would ever be uncovered again. Fortunately, the mosaic continued to inspire, and a chance visitor, Bob Woodward, decided to make an accurate full-size replica, and complete the missing pieces despite having no relevant training.

The first step was for Bob and his brother John to get permission to take thousands of photographs covering every section of the floor, on a grid system. They then developed a technique to project the transparencies of the photos onto a special bench so that each tiny piece of the replica could be laid in the same position as its Roman counterpart. In this way, they could be confident that their replica had a high degree of accuracy.

The original pieces, called tesserae, were cut from local stone. However, because of the difficulty of sourcing and cutting stone tesserae, and the weight, it was decided to use clay pieces as a substitute. Fourteen shades of white, yellow, blue, yellow, and black were carefully colour-matched with clay from local quarries, and twelve tons of it was fired into ten-inch strips. Each strip was then cut into pieces by hand using piano wire cutters. In all, 1.6 million tesserae were needed.

As well as the practical challenges, there was the puzzle of what the missing 40% of the mosaic might have looked like. Despite leaving school at thirteen, Bob found himself, aged forty, studying at The British Museum and Ashmolean Library, and working closely with The Society of Antiquaries and The Royal Commission of Historic Monuments. After several years of painstaking research, he presented his findings to the Institute of Archaeology and at The Getty Centre in Los Angeles to much acclaim

It took ten years to complete the reconstruction project. The finished replica showed The Great Pavement as it may have looked back in 325 CE, when it was laid by the master craftsmen from the Corinium School of Mosaicists in Cirencester. Isn't it amazing?

9

10

A fountain is believed to have been in the centre, as was traditional in grand Roman dining rooms, with a star and fish and sea creatures around it. What appears to be water damage can be seen on the original mosaic in this area.

Orpheus is depicted in the central octagon wearing a cap, tunic and cloak and playing the lyre, with which he charmed birds, fish and animals, to the annoyance of the gods.

11

12

In a circle around him are birds including pheasants, peacocks, and doves (some scratching their heads), plus a hunting dog, close to his master.

13

The most dramatic feature of the mosaic is the animal circle which has eleven beasts: a lion, lioness, wild boar, horse, elephant, gryphon, bear, leopard, stag, and tigress, in amongst trees and other foliage.

14

The gryphon is the only mythical creature, with the body of a lion and the head, wings, and talons of an eagle

15

The elephant has been depicted covered in a decorative net

16

A mask of Neptune, god of the sea, also features. You can see the lobster claws sprouting from his head.

17

The watery theme is also echoed by four nymphs, in varying stages of undress, in the corner spandrels where columns supporting the roof were located.

18

In addition, the mosaic features multiple complex patterns, such as these acanthus scrolls to symbolise the waves of the sea.

19

There are also twenty-four geometric panels outside the central square which display almost all of the standard patterns used by Roman mosaicists. These panels appear symmetrical but are not: each one is unique and full of detail.

On a sunny Sunday afternoon in June 1973, when my father asked me if I wanted to go and see a Roman pavement with him, I said no; I had a book to read instead. It's one of my greatest regrets. The replica is currently in private hands and not on display.

20

2023 marks the fiftieth anniversary of the last unveiling of the original Great Pavement. The grassy Woodchester churchyard is now the closest I can get to the original mosaic, but what better way to toast the anniversary than with a glass of fabulous Orpheus wine from the Woodchester vineyard.

What will be YOUR specialist subject?

- a local landmark
- your best-ever holiday
- a historical figure
- your favourite football manager
- a writer, artist, or composer
- a significant event
- a collection of items
- birds or plants in your garden
- a particular year
- a tradition you keep going
- a musical instrument
- a charitable cause that resonates with you
- your favourite book(s)
- a hobby, interest, or activity
- the business you'd open on the high street
- or abseiling, bee-keeping; carpentry, darts, emu-rearing, fencing, geology, horse-whispering, ice-carving, jade, kite-flying, line dancing, mushrooms, nautical instruments, origami, pigeon-fancying, Queen Anne, railways, shadow puppetry, tulip trees, umbrellas, violinists, wild swimming, X Factor, yeomanry, Zenobia

Stand and deliver!

Select your images (drawings, photos, or PowerPoint slides) and then prepare short captions to go with each. Have a few run-throughs to ensure you can keep to time(ish)

Then be brave for seven minutes and deliver your presentation to a friend, using drawings, photos, or PowerPoint slides.

If you're feeling even braver, record your presentation. Then simply share your love for your specialist subject a little more widely!

You could also work with an older person in your life to help them create a Pecha Kucha or two of their own. What would their specialist subjects be?

8. Wipe that frown

Oh, is that the sound of your doorbell ringing? Who on earth is at the door at this time of day? You'd better go and find out.

Surprise, surprise! There on your doorstep am I, with a bucket and mop in one hand and drill in the other. Harry is standing behind me wielding a can of WD40.

What is on your list of mini-irritations that you would like us to deal with? After you've offered us a nice cup of tea. Yes, a chocolate Hobnob will do nicely. Thank you.

What regularly offends your sensibilities and strikes discord for your sense of sound, sight, or smell?

Could it be...

- ? a creaky cupboard
- ? that stuck drawer
- ? squeaky wheels
- ? the slamming door
- ? catches that don't catch
- ? a tap that drips
- ? a curtain hook that's missing
- ? locks that stick
- ? the damp smell in the corner
- ? clutter in the hall
- ? old paint in the shed
- ? not being able to find what you're looking for?

Whatever it may be, you have three options:

- Carry on as you are, with it continuing to bother you. Remember, however, that your frown will scrunch up your face and contribute to a general feeling of annoyance and tension

- Accept and ignore it. Change your mindset
- Act and address it. It may only need a little time investment.

Now could be the perfect time to develop your DIY skills, before you grow much older.

The Christmas before last, Mum was gifted her first toolbox all of her own. It was about time, as she was eighty-four.

I also received my first power drill which had been top of my wish list, while Santa manhandled an airfryer down the chimney for the BYS, just as he'd been asked.

Here's what I was after that drill for...

We live in an Edwardian house built around 1905. It has a closed-in redbrick porch which faces north, and passing through it each day on my way to work and then back again, was not filling me with joy.

It was a breeding ground for wellies and sturdy shoes, boxes and bags that needed to go to a charity shop, and random items that were en route to the tip: the laundry basket no longer living its best life as the recipient of stained and stinky washing; the vacuum cleaner that had taken its last wheezy breath; the antique lamp that had once graced the 'front parlour' with its fringed shade and pulleys to raise and lower it, until it was promptly pulled out of the ceiling by Lovely Laura on the day we moved in (a quick, cheap and easy way to get the job done).

The porch had also been damp in the past, and a musty smell lingered, ready to greet me with open arms each time I opened the front door.

How could I best use this space? It didn't seem to have much going for it, but I decided to go with its attributes of staying cool all year round, and being quite bright throughout the day, while not receiving any direct sunlight.

- ✔ After getting rid of all the unwanted items in a couple of car trips, I had an empty area to play with. The old metal shoe rack we'd been using had sloping shelves, so was re-purposed as a wine rack, which then freed up space in the kitchen.

- ✔ On the top shelf, I put a plant carry tray, which I'd sprayed silver (channelling memories of Blue Peter). After a bit of experimentation, I found plants which were happy living there all year round and also discovered that the residual dampness disappeared as the plants seemed to draw it in and then didn't need watering so often. The mustiness retreated.

- ✔ The boots and shoes were re-homed on a stand with eight upright prongs (which, upside down, could also double up as a great display stand for large hand puppets,)

- ✔ I got my drill out to put up three lightweight round mirrors from a charity shop. The shape echoes one of the porch windows and the sea-themed stained glass in the others. They remind me of portholes,

- ✔ Excited at the prospect of drilling more holes in the wall. I hung up a few pots with trailing ivy, which seems to enjoy living in these conditions.

My mini-project brings more of a smile than a frown to my face now as I pass through the space. That's good for my facial muscles, as well as my mood, as I head out the door.

I also have some confidence in my emerging drill skills and am grateful to all those experienced DIY-ers on YouTube for their helpful videos.

What are the things around you that keep bringing a furrowed frown to your forehead?

Can you fix them? Yes, maybe you can!

9. YYYs

Well, here we are. Hurtling towards the end of the book. Yes, I know there is a pile of stuff I haven't covered, a pile so large that Grandpa Cliff wouldn't be able to see to the top, even with the help of his humungous binoculars.

Who knows, though, one day there may be a trilogy of books to capture all things old age: Happy, Happier, and Happiest Silver People. I'll give away a bunch of bananas with every box set.

The one area I must cover before we face the final pages is sleep. I've entitled this section YYYs, as it's about what happens to help us reach the ZZZs of slumber.

Sleep, as we know, is incredibly important for our bodies, brains, and general well-being. Around eight hours of quality shut-eye is usually recommended, so we feel refreshed and relaxed the next day.

The quantity of sleep we need may decrease with age, but the quality is still important and dozing off can become more difficult if we are in discomfort, experiencing anxiety or feeling down. Building an effective night-time routine may take a little while, but we could feel the benefit for many years to come.

Here are some suggestions for winding down before bed:

- ✔ Ditch caffeine in the afternoon, and switch to camomile, turmeric, or peppermint tea. Stop drinking around an hour before you plan to go to bed

- ✔ Also, switch off your screen an hour before, or pop on a pair of glasses which block blue light

- ✔ Set up your room in advance: pre-cool by opening a window, pull down your black-out blinds, pick out your clothes for the next day – and, in winter, put them inside out on a radiator

- ✔ Choose an ambient light setting using a special, inexpensive bulb with an app or remote control. Now is not the time to experiment with the novelty disco ball effect

- ✔ Try a hot water bottle. My love affair with hotties began as a student in Scotland when I bought a cracked stone pig from a second-hand shop. Unfortunately, I had to make sure it was upright in the bed, or it would dribble everywhere

  Nowadays, I take a rubber hottie to bed every night, except in the height of summer, when I should try filling it with chilled water to transform it into a coldie

- ✔ Set out a Shakti mat on your bed, ready for a pre-sleep de-stress. It may look like a modern version of a bed of nails, but it's designed to relieve muscle tension and improve your circulation by pushing on your pressure points, and it works. I lie on it while I'm reading, nice and warm under my duvet.

As you drift off, consider the appreciation we should show to Edmund (Ted) Blanket, a fourteenth-century weaver in Bristol.

One crispy cold night back in 1343, Ted ran out of firewood, but, fortunately, his grey cells were still firing. He laid out on his bed some unfinished, loosely woven woollen cloth which he'd brought home with him, and he and Mrs. Blanket had a toasty night's sleep.

News of this invention travelled fast and generated queues of potential customers - queues even longer than for a 1970s Harrods sale. Eventually, even the King, Edward III, ordered a couple of the woollen novelties, meaning Ted's fortune was made. Ted is now sleeping soundly in St Stephen's Church, just off the city centre. I do hope he is snuggled up tight in his favourite blanket.

- ? How could you adjust your bedtime routine to prepare yourself better for a refreshing night's sleep?

- ? Which new pre-sleep habits might you need to adopt, and which old habits might you need to break to stand you in good stead as you grow older?

10. ZZZs

And finally, we have it: sleep, glorious sleep.

If I were ever on Mastermind, surely sleep would be my specialist-selected subject.

Although, if I'm strictly accurate, it's lack of sleep which is my area of personal expertise. One of the effects of Lovely Laura's condition is the inability to produce melatonin and get herself off to the land of Nod. She has medication to help, which sometimes works, works partially, or doesn't appear to work at all.

My specialism is based on fourteen years of chronic interrupted sleep. When you may be woken at any moment by the light being switched on or a noise which means your presence is required. When there is no option of catching up as and when you need to, when you have to carry on functioning and staying on high alert throughout the following day. It's clear to me why sleep deprivation has been used as an instrument of torture for centuries.

What's the effect of utter exhaustion from lack of sleep?

It can lead to cognitive impairment as the neuronal networks of the brain are disrupted, making it harder to think and also remember. There are also possible links to anxiety, stress, and depression, plus weight gain, and a possible connection to dementia in later life.

This was the impact of lack of sleep on me:

- My brain fog was more like a 'pea-souper' which lifted rarely. I made errors, got dates and numbers wrong, and forgot what I'd already done. But at least I was consistent. When I re-did something for the second time, I would produce something that was almost identical to the first.

- I had lapses of memory, both immediate and longer term. There are huge gaps in what I remember from those years: conversations, events, even people I used to interact with regularly

- I suffered impaired judgement and had difficulty making decisions, with simple choices sometimes becoming overwhelming

- Exhaustion sometimes made me physically sick, once just moments after I'd been facilitating some customer service training with a group of colleagues

- Road rage could envelop me without warning. I'd find myself leaving burnt rubber on the road as I followed drivers who were using their phones at the wheel, in the hope of confronting them. Fortunately, they always lost me in the leafy back streets.

- And once, on the way to work, I was woken by the driver in the car behind tooting at me; I'd fallen asleep at the wheel. With my foot drooping onto the brake, luckily.

- My appearance? My skin showed my tiredness and I put on weight. My preference had always been for savoury foods, but now I craved sweeter items to quickly boost my energy and cheer me up. The changes in the way I looked affected my confidence and my desire to go out in public

- Overall, I was irritable, unreasonable, impatient, tearful. And just so unspeakably weary. It meant I was not always a nice person to be around and, if that was your experience of me, I am exceedingly sorry.

So never mind that old saying about living life to the full and doing your sleeping when you're dead. Getting enough quality sleep and developing good bedtime habits sooner rather than later is a top-ranking priority.

Here are my suggestions for a good night's sleep, based on years of sleeping too lightly or not at all myself, and also of trying to get Lovely Laura off to sleep.

After setting in place the YYYs as outlined in preparatory steps in the previous section, here's what you can take you over into the ZZZs...

- ✔ A comfortable mattress is a key bit of kit. If you're going to invest in anything, put your money into that (not literally)

- ✔ Choose bedding which doesn't bother you, by catching on your toenails, for example. Whatever the texture, colour, and design of the fabric, it needs to be right for you

- ✔ If you are restless at night, consider a weighted blanket. There's been a trend for them for a while, but what I'm talking about is not off-the-shelf; it's one that is appropriate for your size and weight. Lovely Laura was recommended one by a great charity called Brainwave about fifteen years ago. Putting it on top of her duvet had a positive impact in terms of increasing her sense of security and reducing the need to fidget.

- ✔ Bed socks can also stop your feet from exploring the bed – but don't wear them all night every night, as your feet need time to breathe.

  A long-standing mystery is where Lovely Laura's bed socks actually are, as the drawer is full of odd ones. Are they like the eels which return to the wide Sargasso Sea to find a new mate? Or perhaps they have retired to be near other single socks on Dobby's grave in the unspoilt dunes of West Wales? I do know, though, that there is one starry pink one behind the Afghanistan display at the Dorset Tank Museum.

- ✔ Foot stretches in bed were recommended to me by my acupuncturist, as they may be holding tension after working hard all day, Flex your toes up as far as you can, then curl them down five times. Follow that with five ankle rotations to the right, then five to the left. Your hooves should now be ready to rest.

- ✔ If you have a blocked nose, try Breathe Right strips to keep your nasal passages clear. You won't be a sleeping beauty, but you won't care

- ✔ My mum's top tip is a little dab of Vic under your nose, whether you have a cold or not. It's the soothing smell which sends her off into oblivion.

And, for my grand finale, here are my 100% guaranteed ways to get to sleep - after you've opened or closed the window, minimised all noise and light, checked you've locked the back door, and been to the loo once again.

Plan A:

I heard this tip on the radio a few years ago and would love to thank the person who was sharing it. Because it works! Who knew that the magic number for sleep is twenty-seven?

Count backwards slowly in your head from twenty-seven. Focus on each number as you go. I rarely reach one; in the unlikely event that you do, try it again.

Plan B:

If Plan A isn't working, let's roll out Plan B. Think through your day in minute detail, from when you woke up, through to when you opened your eyes, switched off the alarm clock, and then got up, and what you did next, and what came after that. Visualise every moment, frame by frame by frame....

...and then you should wake up a few hours later! When I've had to revert to Plan B, I've never got beyond recalling the first hour of my day.

Sweet silver dreams...

Another beginning

Tomorrow, tomorrow

Tomorrow, tomorrow

So, here we are at the end of the book already. It seems only a moment ago we were at the introductions stage, and now it's nearly time to say farewell.

I hope the questions I asked back at the start have resonated with you, as they did for me.

I hope you've stimulated your senses, exercised your silver cells, and found magic in the mundane.

I hope you've found points to ponder and identified where you could invest time and energy to prepare yourself for later life.

I hope you may be planning to push yourself out of the nesting zone of older comfort, to be creative in new ways, and to be thankful, kind, and well-connected to the world around you.

Mostly though, I hope you're feeling more positive as you look to the horizon with your gargantuan binoculars, towards tomorrow, and tomorrow, and tomorrow...

> **What you do today can improve all your tomorrows**
>
> Ralph Marston

Just before you go, let me save my manuscript, put my new yellow glasses down in a random place, and quickly pop to the loo...

Acknowledgements

I have so many people to thank. There are those who have raised me and praised me, encouraged me and supported me, listened to me and laughed with me, and stayed around when the going got tough.

An extra-special, sterling silver thank you also goes to:

- The older generations of inspiring people whom I have been so very fortunate to have as grandparents, aunts and uncles, in-laws, and family friends.
- Simon Scarborough, whose positive feedback planted the seed of an idea, which later blossomed into Happy Silver People.
- Emily at You Hair for transforming me into a real silver person.
- My colleague Doug, who enthusiastically became my ever first YouTube subscriber - and to those who followed his example!
- The intrepid interviewees who agreed to appear in my YouTube videos: Kevin, Melsia, Roger, Steph, Deb, Debbie, Julia, and the lovely, late Pete Wells.
- The people who kindly wrote endorsements for me as the author of this book: Liz Davies, Paul Kinvig and Mandy May (who also took me to see a joyful Tom Jones on a perfect summer's evening).
- Best-selling author, Michael Heppell, for helping me realise I wanted to write a book, and then giving me the confidence to believe that I could. As he says, "It's not the book you read that will change your life, it's the book you write." Without his guidance, encouragement, and support through three Write That Book masterclasses, you would not be reading this.
- Fellow members of the writing groups and Team 17. What a brilliant bunch of people you are. There are too many of you to list here, but a special mention for keeping me on track goes to my tenacious writing buddies Lynne and Anne, as well as Sue, Jaki, Fiona x 2, Gayle, Kath, Steve, Lorna and Helen, members of top team #Dynamics, and Karl, the most constructive of coaches.

- The fabulous members of the Happy Silver People Facebook group – whose e-company I have greatly enjoyed.
- Sue Trusler and Jaki Lewis-Thompson who so kindly contributed to this book; Michaela Deasy for refreshing the Happy Silver People logo; and my cousin Mark for digging out the mosaic photos.
- Matthew Bird in the Land of Smiles for his inexhaustible patience and good humour while typesetting this book and its cover.
- Pam Linham and Simon Siddall for writing *Bob: the Other Builder* in 2006. Having Dad's biography to refer to has been invaluable.
- Harry Redknapp for being so supportive of my endeavours and for generously sharing his thoughts for the foreword to this book. I have no doubt at all that he will always be nice!
- My marvelous mum for being the kindest of critics, right from day one, and for even offering to buy her own copy of the book. I just wish Dad could have read it too.
- My ever-thoughtful brother, James, who got me enthused about smiley bananas. How lucky I am to be his lovely sister.
- Rob for his ongoing encouragement and unfailing behind-the-scenes back-up, and Lovely Laura for being the most wonderful and welcome distraction from writing.
- Everyone who has helped us to keep Laura safe and smiling, especially Charlene and Tracey, and also Jane who has looked after us at our second home (the garden centre) at weekends for many years.
- Mr. Pendock who, many years ago, gave my parents an annual subscription to Readers' Digest. Each month I read those magazines avidly, as they ignited my interest in the world around me.

> I feel a very unusual sensation —
> if it is not indigestion, I think it must be gratitude
>
> Benjamin Disraeli

Who's Who?

Dad
Hugh
James
Laura
Mum
Rachel
Rob
Robert

About the Author

Rachel is an ordinary person who has had an unusual life.

Born in Bristol, she has been a big sister to three brothers, but not all at the same time. In 1973, her football-mad brother, Robert, was diagnosed with cancer and sadly lost his fight just before he turned twelve. Her cuddlesome baby brother Hugh, born a year later with Down's Syndrome, suffered a fatal heart attack when he was four.

Rachel's father, in his forties, changed the direction of their lives by founding the CLIC charity (Cancer and Leukaemia in Childhood - later CLIC Sargent and now Young Lives vs Cancer) to support children with cancer and their families. He was instrumental in raising over £100m for various charities during his lifetime, and this led to some surreal situations for Rachel, such as coming home to find Kevin Keegan kicking a football around on the front lawn and chatting with Mr. Gorbachev on his private plane.

For thirty-five years, Rachel has worked in international education, living in the UK and also overseas for thirteen years. She met her husband, Rob, when they were both working in Syria twenty-five years ago. Travel stopped, however, when their beautiful daughter, Laura, was diagnosed with severe learning difficulties.

Rachel currently lives in Bournemouth where she works full-time, as well as being a charity ambassador and a board member for Bournemouth's Town Centre Business Improvement District and the International Education Association. She has recently started paddleboarding and playing tennis, and may be persuaded by Rob to go camping again one day. She visits her hometown to see her mother and brother James when she can.

With her sixtieth birthday on the horizon, Rachel decided to look into how she could prepare for older age and share her ideas with others through Happy Silver People.

Writing this book has helped fill the void created by Laura moving into supported living, and has been a great excuse for not doing much cleaning.